to Andrea + Jackie
love Grandpa +
Grandma Wall
Easter 1985

# BIBLE STORIES to Live by

by

V. Gilbert Beers and Ronald A. Beers

Illustrations by Reint De Jonge

HERE'S LIFE PUBLISHERS, INC.
San Bernardino, California

# TO PARENTS AND TEACHERS

You are part of a growing number of parents and teachers who are concerned about their children. Many are searching for a way for their children to learn "old-fashioned" moral and spiritual values such as honesty, courage, love, self-control and reverence. These time-honored values may seem old-fashioned, but they are as contemporary as today's child who is under construction, and who will become tomorrow's Christian leader.

Each story in this book focuses on one of the familiar values so important for our children. These values are seen at work in the lives of Bible-time people. Sometimes a story shows how that person failed to show love, or reverence, and why that hurt. At other times the story shows how a person showed love or reverence, and why that worked.

Questions help your child understand how each moral or spiritual value can be applied today in his or her own life.

In the back you will find an alphabetical guide to the moral and spiritual values taught in this book.

BIBLE STORIES TO LIVE BY
by V. Gilbert Beers and Ronald A. Beers

Illustrations by Reint De Jonge

Published by
HERE'S LIFE PUBLISHERS, INC.
P. O. Box 1576
San Bernardino, CA 92402, USA

Library of Congress Catalogue Card 82-084616
ISBN 0-89840-044-9
HLP Product No. 95-050-1
© Copyright 1983 Here's Life Publishers, Inc.

Adapted from: *The Kleuterbijbel*
        Originally published by: Boekencentrum B.V.
                Scheveningseweg 72
                25717 KX 's-Gravenhage
                The Netherlands

Typeset: Omega/Lucas Graphics, Tarzana, California, USA

Printed in The Netherlands.

# CONTENTS

# God Makes a Wonderful World

## A Story about ORDERLINESS

In the beginning, there was nothing . . . nothing but God. No world had been made, no sun, moon, or stars. There were no birds or animals or plants or trees. Instead, there was nothing but darkness and empty space.

But God had a wonderful plan. He called it creation. God would fill the dark empty spaces with beautiful things. He would make these beautiful things from nothing.

At the right time, God began His wonderful work. "Let there be light!" God said. Light appeared in the dark skies and the darkness hid from it. God called the light places day and the dark places night.

"Let there be a sky above and an earth below!" God said. The earth formed into a beautiful ball and the sky rose above it. A clear horizon appeared where the earth and the sky met.

"Let the waters gather together and the dry land appear," God said. The waters moved together to form the seas and the dry land appeared, with mountains and valleys and fields.

"Let grass and plants and trees grow upon the dry land," God said. The land burst forth with beautiful flowers and bushes, trees and plants. God must have smiled at the wonder of it all.

God spoke and the sun warmed the earth. He spoke and the moon appeared. One by one stars twinkled in the skies.

"Let birds and fish and animals appear," God said. The quiet skies broke forth in birdsong and the still waters sparkled with fish. Animals ran across the hills. The earth was a garden of beauty and harmony. Everything was exactly where it should be, and everything worked together exactly the way it should, like the parts of a beautiful watch. And God saw that it was good!

## THINK

1. Think about the world that God made. Why do you think God made it? Why didn't it just happen? 2. The world keeps better time in its movements than the finest watch. Why didn't this just happen? 3. Think about the beautiful flowers that come from seeds. Why didn't this just happen?

## LEARN

From this story you learn about God's orderliness. God put everything in the right place. When the world gets out of place, it is because we messed it up. God didn't.

## DO

Draw a big circle. This is the world. Now draw in and around the circle some things that God made. Don't forget the sun, moon, stars, trees, animals, and people.

# A Garden Home

## *A Story about* HAPPINESS

The whole earth was a beautiful garden, with sights and sounds and smells blending together. God was pleased with His work. He was pleased to see how well everything worked together. But it was too wonderful to keep for Himself alone. God planned to share it with someone—someone like Himself.

One place was more beautiful than all others. God created a man, named him Adam, and put him in charge of this beautiful garden called Eden. There wasn't much for Adam to do in Eden, for everything worked together the way it should.

One day God brought each kind of animal to Adam so that he could name them. Then He put Adam in charge of the animals. Adam was glad for the animals, but something—someone—was missing. God knew who this someone was, and He knew what to do.

God put Adam to sleep and then took a rib from his side and made a woman. He brought the woman to Adam to become his wife.

Together Adam and his wife lived happily in Eden. Why shouldn't they be happy? What more could they need?

Adam and Eve not only had everything they needed, but they also had everything they wanted. Then God told them about something they could not have, something they should not want.

"You may eat anything in the Garden of Eden except one fruit," God told them. "If you eat the fruit from the tree of the knowledge of good and evil you will die."

Adam and Eve listened carefully to God. As long as they obeyed Him, they lived happily in their garden home.

## THINK

1. Think about the things Adam and Eve had. What more did they need? What more should they have wanted? 2. Now think about the things you have. What more do you need? What more should you want?

## LEARN

From this story, you learn about happiness. As long as Adam and Eve obeyed God, they were happy. As long as you obey God and your parents, you can be happy.

## DO

Do you remember the last time you felt unhappy? Ask yourself what happened just before that. Did you disobey God or your parents? The next time you are unhappy, ask quickly if you have disobeyed.

# Adam and Eve Are Tempted

*A Story about* TEMPTATION

"**D**id God REALLY say that?" the serpent asked Eve.

"God said we may eat anything in the garden except this fruit," Eve answered. "If we eat this, we will die."

"You won't die," Satan, the serpent said. "When you eat this fruit, you will see things you never saw before. You will know the difference between good and evil."

When Satan tempts, he tells little half truths. He was half right and half wrong. Adam and Eve would not lie down and die and be buried. But when they disobeyed God, sin would come between them and God and would keep them from being good friends with God. This kind of death is much worse than the other.

Eve listened to Satan's words. They did not seem half true. She thought they were all true. So she ate some of the fruit and gave some to Adam to eat too.

Satan's half truth was right. Adam and Eve did not lie down and die. But something died inside. They knew they had sinned against God. They knew that sin had come between them and God and had spoiled their beautiful friendship with Him. They were ashamed, so ashamed that they made fig-leaf clothes to wear and they hid from God. They did not want to see God or talk with Him. But God found them and spoke to them.

"Because you did not obey Me, you must leave the Garden of Eden," God told Adam and Eve. "You must work hard for a living. You will have sorrow and pain." Adam and Eve were sorry now that they had disobeyed God and had sinned. They were sorry that they had spoiled their friendship with God. This was worse than dying!

## DO

Write two words on a piece of paper—EVE and PRAY. Next time you are tempted to do something wrong, take this paper from your pocket or book and look at it. It will remind you of the trouble Eve had when she was tempted. It will remind you to pray and ask God to help you.

## THINK

1. What spoiled the friendship that Adam and Eve had with God? 2. Why did Adam and Eve eat this fruit when they already had all that they needed? 3. How have you been tempted? What were you tempted to do? Why did you think you needed this? 4. Next time you are tempted, pray!

## LEARN

From this story, you learn that you are tempted to do things God does not want you to do, and these things will hurt your friendship with God.

9

# Cain Kills Abel

*A Story about* JEALOUSY

As time passed Adam and Eve had two sons. Cain grew up and became a grain farmer. Abel grew up and became a shepherd.

These two young men were quite different. Abel pleased God but Cain did not. Both young men gave offerings to God, but they did not give the same way.

Cain saw that God rewarded Abel more than him. God was more pleased with Abel's offerings because He was more pleased with Abel and the way he lived for God. This made Cain more jealous each day.

Jealousy has a way of eating the smile from our faces and the laughter from our hearts. That's what happened to Cain. His face grew bitter and angry, showing what was in his heart.

"Why do you look that way?" God asked Cain. "If you please Me, I will accept you. If you keep on sinning, it will control you."

That is exactly what happened. One day Cain's jealousy ate too deep into his heart. While he and Abel were working in the fields, Cain, in a fit of anger, struck Abel and killed him.

Cain had lost control of himself. Jealousy took over. On that sad day, God punished Cain by sending him away from his home, his family, and from God Himself. Lonely and afraid, Cain ran, and he kept on running—running away from the terrible thing jealousy made him do, and running away from God.

## THINK

1. What terrible thing did Cain do to Abel? 2. Why did he do this? 3. How did jealousy cause him to kill his brother? 4. What do you do when you are jealous? Remember Cain and Abel.

## LEARN

From this story you learn how jealousy eats away at our hearts and minds and makes us do things we should not do.

## DO

Are you jealous of someone now? Is someone jealous of you? Tonight before you go to bed, pray and ask God to help you or your jealous friend.

# Noah and the Great Flood

*A Story about* OBEDIENCE

Many years passed after the time of Cain and Abel. People forgot about God and lived the way they wanted to live, not the way God wanted them to live. By the time of Noah, almost everyone was living sad, sinful lives. Only Noah and his family pleased God.

God was not pleased with Noah's wicked neighbors. He was sorry that He had made them. So God said, "I will destroy these people and their animals." Only Noah and his family would be spared.

"Make an ark, a large boat," God told Noah. "I will send a flood upon the earth. It will destroy people and animals. But you and your family will be safe in the ark."

God told Noah to bring two of each kind of animal, a male and a female, into this ark. Through them, all future animals would be born.

The ark would be as big as seventy-five houses, much longer than a football field, and as tall as a three-story building. Think of the work Noah and his sons must do to make such a boat!

Noah and his family were discouraged many times as they cut trees, sawed them into beams or boards, and hammered them into place on the ark. They wanted to quit when neighbors laughed at them for building this boat far from the ocean.

But Noah obeyed God and did all that God told him to do. For a hundred and twenty years he kept on cutting, sawing, carrying, hammering, and listening to his neighbors. He kept on obeying God, even when he wanted to quit.

But the day came when Noah and his family were glad that they had obeyed God. The rains fell and the waters roared up from the depths of the seas. For forty days and forty nights, the rain came down in torrents. All who were outside the ark were drowned. Inside the ark, Noah, his family, and the animals were safe and dry.

What a sad day that would have been if Noah had not obeyed God!

## THINK

1. What would you think if God told you to build a big boat at the edge of your town? What must Noah have thought? But he did it because God said to do it. 2. What do you think when your parents ask you to do something? Do you obey without grumbling? Should you?

## LEARN

From this story, you learn that it pays to obey God. It pays also to obey your parents.

## DO

Pretend you are a mother or father and your pet is your child. Ask you "child" to come for dinner, or do something that will help him. Do you expect him to obey?

# Noah Thanks God

## *A Story about* PROMISES

Living on the ark was not much fun for Noah and his family. Each day they fed the animals, cleaned the stalls, and did the other chores. They could not go out into the back yard or go next door to see the neighbors. There was no back yard and there were no neighbors. There was no one else in the world and nowhere else to go.

Noah and his family could not even see outside the ark. The only window was too small and too high for them to look outside.

But Noah and his family did not complain about the chores or the other problems. They were safe and dry inside the ark. Their neighbors were not, for they were drowned in the flood.

The months passed slowly on the ark. They had time to think about the things that God had done. How thankful they were that they had believed God's promise that a flood would come. How thankful they were that they had believed God when He told them to build this boat. And how thankful they were that they had believed God's promise to save Noah and his family if they would obey Him and build the ark.

At last it was time for Noah and his family to leave the ark. A new world smiled as they stepped outside. The sun never seemed brighter or the trees and flowers more beautiful. The animals, penned up for a year inside the ark, romped and played upon the hills, and the birds soared high into the skies.

Noah and his family made an altar. They thanked God for saving them. They thanked God for keeping His promises.

God had another promise for Noah. "Never again will I destroy My people and animals with a flood over all the earth," He said. Then God sent a beautiful rainbow. It was a sign, a way to help Noah, and us, remember that God always keeps His promises.

## THINK

1. What did God promise if Noah built the ark? How did God keep His promise to Noah? 2. Think what would have happened if Noah had not believed God's promise. What may have been different?

## LEARN

From this story, you learn that God always keeps His promises. Since God keeps His promises, you should keep yours.

## DO

Look up Romans 4:21 in your Bible. CAN God do what He promises? Now look up I Kings 8:56. WILL God do what He promises?

15

# Abram Goes to a New Land

## *A Story about* OBEDIENCE

Do you remember hearing about Abraham and Sarah? When they were younger, they lived in a land near Ur, and were called Abram and Sarai. The neighbors at Ur seemed like decent, well-to-do people, but they built pyramid-shaped towers, called ziggurats, where they worshipped strange gods.

God spoke to Abram and told him to go to a land far away. So Abram and his entire family left Ur and moved toward this new land. Along the way they stopped at a place called Haran, far to the north. There the family settled down and lived until Abram's father Terah died.

Then God spoke to Abram again. "Leave your home and family here at Haran, and go to a land I will show you," God told him. "In this new land you will have many children, and your descendants will become a great nation. Through you all families on earth will be blessed."

Moving to a new land and living among strange people was not easy in Abram's time. It would have been easier for Abram to stay in Haran and live the rest of his life with family and friends.

But Abram obeyed God. With Sarai, his nephew Lot, and all his possessions, Abram moved across the many miles to the land of Canaan, the land where God led him. Travel was hard, mile upon mile swaying wearily on camels, or walking across the dustry trails which were the only roads of that time.

Travel was slow, too, for Abram and his people could go no faster than the young lambs and calves of their flocks and herds. But no matter how hard, or how slowly they had to move, Abram obeyed God and went where God told him to go.

When Abram and Sarai arrived at last in Canaan, God spoke to them again. "I will give this land to your descendants," God promised. Abram believed God and built an altar, one of many he would build in Canaan. Upon this altar, Abram offered gifts to God, showing that he would obey God completely, no matter where He would lead.

## THINK

1. Think how hard it was for Abram and Sarai to move to a new land. Why did they go to all this trouble? 2. Do you think Abram and Sarai were glad they obeyed God? Why? 3. Are you glad when you obey God and do what He says? How would you feel if you didn't?

## LEARN

From this story, you learn about OBEDIENCE to God. Abram obeyed God, even when it would have been much easier not to obey.

## DO

Did you obey your parents the last time one of them asked you to do something? If you did, you were happy, weren't you? But if you didn't, you were sad. Put a sheet of paper in your room. Each time you obey, draw a small smiling face on the paper. Each time you do not obey, draw a small sad face on the paper. How many happy faces, or sad faces, do you have by bedtime tonight?

17

# God Takes Care of Hagar

*A Story about* PROVIDING

For many years God promised Abraham and Sarah a son. But as they grew older past the time when people have babies, they wondered about God's promise and became more anxious with each passing year. One day Sarah thought she would wait no longer. She urged Abraham to live with her servant girl Hagar so that he could have a baby through her. Sarah would pretent that Hagar's son was hers.

Sarah's foolish plan soon went wrong. When Hagar had a son, and named him Ishmael, Sarah grew jealous and angry, and began to be mean to Hagar.

At last Sarah had a son and named his Isaac. But she grew even more jealous of Hagar now and nagged Abraham to send Hagar and Ishmael away. "Your heir must be my son Isaac, not Ishmael!" Sarah insisted.

Abraham worried and wondered what he should do until God spoke to him. "Do what Sarah wants," God said. "I will make a great nation of each of your sons."

With great sorrow Abraham sent Hagar and Ishmael to live in the hot dry wilderness. Before long, when her water was gone, Hagar sat down and cried, sure that her son would soon die.

But God saw Hagar in her time of trouble and showed her a well of water. Eagerly Hagar filled her water pot and tenderly gave her son Ishmael a drink. His life, and hers, were spared. God had provided!

Through the years, God continued to provide for Hagar and Ishmael as they lived in that place. God kept his promise too, for Ishmael grew to become the head of a great nation.

## THINK

1. How did God provide for Hagar and Ishmael in the wilderness? 2. What would have happened if God had not sent His angel to show Hagar a well of water? 3. What does God provide for you each day? Can you name five important things?

## LEARN

From this story you learn how God provides. He takes care of us each day, as He did Hagar and Ishmael.

## DO

What five things did you list that God provides? Will you thank God now for each one of them?

# Abraham Offers Isaac

## *A Story about* TRUST

"Take your son Isaac to the land of Moriah," God told Abraham. "Offer him there as a burnt offering."

Abraham could hardly believe what he heard. "Isaac? A burnt offering? Why?" Why would God tell Abraham to offer his son, the son for whom he and Sarah had waited so many years? Abraham could not think of a reason why. But he trusted God completely. He would do whatever God told him to do.

Surely Abraham loved Isaac as much as any father loved his son. He and Sarah had waited and prayed for this son for such a long time. While they waited and prayed, God kept promising that he would be born. Abraham kept trusting God to keep His promise. At last Isaac was born when Abraham was a hundred years old.

Imagine a hundred-year-old man picking up his first baby! Think of the tears that came to his eyes and the smile that came upon his face.

As Isaac grew up, he and Abraham took care of their sheep together. They fixed their tents together. And they did so many other things that fathers and sons do together.

Now Abraham must give up this son. How could he do it? He did not know. But he would do what God said because he trusted Him to do what was right.

The next morning Abraham headed toward Moriah with Isaac, two young servant boys, and wood for the fire. On the third day, Abraham saw the place where they were going. Leaving the servant boys at the foot of the mountain, Abraham and Isaac went up to the place where the offering was to be made. By this time Isaac began to wonder. "Where is the lamb for the offering?" he asked his father.

"God will provide," Abraham answered. Abraham still trusted God to provide some way to keep him from offering his beloved son. Still waiting for God's other way, Abraham laid the wood on the altar, placed Isaac upon it, and lifted his knife to kill him.

Suddenly God called to Abraham, "Stop! Do not hurt Isaac! I know now that you trust Me completely." Then God showed Abraham a ram caught in some bushes.

"You have trusted Me completely," God said to Abraham. "Because you did, I will bless you and your descendants in wonderful ways." Abraham was glad that he had trusted God.

## THINK

1. What did God ask Abraham to do? 2. How did Abraham show that he trusted God completely? 3. What do you do to show God that you trust Him? 4. When you read the Bible, whose book are you reading? Why should you do what it says?

## LEARN

From this story you learn how Abraham trusted God completely, even when it seemed impossible to do it.

## DO

Look up the following verses in the Bible which tell you about trust: Psalm 52:8; Psalm 56:3,4; Proverbs 3:5,6. Ask how you can trust God more because of what you learn here.

21

# Jacob Steals His Brother's Blessing

## A Story about HONESTY

Now that Isaac was old and blind, he decided to give his blessing to his older son Esau. This was very important to a son, for it had to do with leading the family when the father died.

While Esau was his father's favorite son, Jacob was his mother's favorite. She heard about the blessing and made plans for Jacob to get it instead of Esau.

"I heard your father tell Esau to hunt a wild animal and cook it for him," Rebekah told Jacob. "We must cook some goat meat while he is gone. You will take it to your father and he will give you his blessing."

Jacob was afraid, but he did what his mother said. Then he put goat hair on his neck and hands so they would feel more like Esau's hairy skin.

As soon as the meat was cooked, Jacob took it to his father's tent. "My father," Jacob said when he went in. "Who is it?" Isaac asked.

"I am Esau, your firstborn," Jacob lied. "Eat my meat and give me your blessing."

Isaac was suspicious. He thought the voice was Jacob's, but he was too blind to see who it was. So he called Jacob to him and felt his hands and neck.

"The voice is Jacob's, but the hands are Esau's," Isaac said. "Are you really my son Esau?"

Jacob had to lie again. "I am," he said. When he said that, Isaac ate the meat and gave Jacob the blessing, thinking he was Esau. Then he settled down to rest as Jacob quickly left the tent. Jacob had deceived his father and had stolen his brother's blessing.

Jacob had just left when Esau came into the tent with his meat. "Eat my meat and give me your blessing," Esau said to his father.

Isaac sat up, surprised at what he heard. "Who are you?" he asked.

Now Esau was surprised. "I'm your son Esau," he answered.

When Isaac told Esau what had happened, Esau gave a loud, bitter cry. "Bless me too!" he begged.

"Your brother has stolen your blessing," said Isaac. "He is now head of the family and you must serve him."

Esau was so angry that he vowed that he would kill his brother Jacob. Of course Jacob and his mother heard about that and it soon became clear that Jacob must go away from home to live. He had stolen his father's blessing but now he could not live with his family.

## THINK

1. What did Jacob do that was not honest? 2. How did this affect his family? 3. Which family members were hurt by Jacob's dishonesty? How?

## LEARN

From this story you learn that people often get what they want by being dishonest, but someone usually gets hurt.

## DO

Using a sheet of construction paper, make a green tree. Cut out nine pieces of fruit from other colors on construction paper. Now turn to Galatians 5:22 and write one type of "fruit" on each of these. Put them on your tree. Whenever you are tempted to lie or be dishonest, look at the fruit. Ask which fruit you want but feel you will not have because of the lie or dishonesty.

23

# Jacob Marries Rachel

*A Story about* LOVE

"Where are you from?" Jacob asked the shepherds who sat talking by a well.

"Haran," the shepherds answered. Jacob smiled. At last he had found someone who could show him the way to Haran. He had come hundreds of miles to find his uncle Laban who lived there. Somewhere in Laban's family Jacob hoped to find the girl he would marry.

"Do you know Laban?" Jacob asked.

"Yes, of course we know him," said the shepherds. "Here comes his daughter Rachel with the family sheep."

Jacob watched the young lady with the sheep. So this was Laban's daughter. How beautiful she was. Could this be the girl he would marry? If so, would he love her?

Jacob wanted to be alone with Rachel when he met her. Why did those shepherds have to be there?

"Why don't you water your sheep and get them back to pasture?" Jacob asked the shepherds.

"We don't do things that way," said the shepherds. Besides, they wanted to see what would happen.

By this time, Rachel had come to the well with her sheep. Jacob wasn't sure how to introduce himself, so he ran to the well, rolled the stone from it and began to water her sheep. Then Jacob told Rachel that he was her cousin, the son of her Aunt Rebekah. He was so happy that he kissed Rachel and began to cry.

Jacob fell in love with Rachel. He loved her so much that he worked 14 years for her father so that he could marry her. Don't you think that Rachel must have loved Jacob for doing this?

## THINK

1. When you love someone, how much are you willing to do for them? 2. How much did Jacob do to show his love for Rachel? 3. How do you think Rachel felt about Jacob because he worked 14 years to marry her? 4. What special things do you do for those you love most?

## LEARN

From this story, you learn that you should do much more than is expected for someone you love.

## DO

Cut seven small cards, one for each day this week. Write on each something special you would like to do for your mother, father, brother, sister, or someone else you love. Put the day of the week on the card and give it to this person. Be sure to do that special thing on the day you promise. And be sure not to promise something you will not do.

# Joseph Is Sold as a Slave

## *A Story about* JEALOUSY

Everyone knew that Joseph was Jacob's favorite son. Jacob did not try to hide this. Of course this made Joseph's other brothers jealous. They grew even more jealous when Jacob gave Joseph a beautiful robe that was much better than theirs.

One night Joseph dreamed that he and his brothers were binding stalks of grain into sheaves. Joseph's sheaf of grain suddenly stood up and his brothers' sheaves bowed down before it. Joseph told his brothers about this dream and their jealousy turned to hatred. "Do you think you will rule over us some day?" they complained.

This jealous hatred kept troubling the brothers, but they did nothing about it. Then Joseph dreamed another dream. This time the sun, moon and eleven stars bowed down before him. Joseph told this dream to his brothers and his father.

Joseph's father Jacob was disturbed about the dream. "What is this?" he asked. "Will your mother and I and your brothers bow to the ground before you?" Of course the brothers' jealousy grew increasingly worse.

One day Joseph's brothers were taking care of the family sheep many miles north of their home. "Go find them, and make sure that all is well," Jacob told Joseph.

Jacob should never have sent his teenage son to visit the older brothers in a place that far from home. He should have known how jealous they were. But Jacob, like any father, could not think that one brother would hurt another.

When Joseph's brothers saw him coming, they talked angrily with one another. Their jealous hatred had been kept to themselves. Now it was turning the brothers into Joseph's enemies.

"Let's kill him," they said. "We will dump him into a cistern and tell our father a wild animal ate him. That will stop those dreams!"

Reuben, the oldest brother was afraid. He tried to stop the others. "We must not kill him," he said. "Let's just put him into the cistern like a prison instead." Reuben hoped to come back and rescue Joseph.

As soon as Joseph reached the brothers, they grabbed him, tore off his beautiful robe, and threw him into an empty cistern. Then they sat down to eat their lunch.

Before they could eat, the brothers saw a caravan of traders coming. Then Judah had an idea. "Let's sell Joseph to those traders," he said. "Then we will not have to kill him.

The brothers knew that Joseph would suffer much as a slave. He would probably die before long, as many slaves did. But they sold him anyway.

As the caravan disappeared beyond the horizon, the brothers must have wondered what they had done. But it was too late now. They had sold their own brother as a slave. Their jealousy would make them all suffer.

## THINK

1. Why were Joseph's brothers jealous? 2. What did Jacob do to make them jealous? What did Joseph do to make the jealous? 3. How did their jealousy make Joseph suffer? 4. How do you think the brothers suffered after Joseph was sold?

## LEARN

From this story you learn that jealousy causes people to do terrible things.

## DO

Write down the name of someone who has done something, or has something that makes you jealous. Talk with your mother or father to see what you should do about this.

# Joseph In Prison

*A Story about* FAITHFULNESS

When Joseph arrived in Egypt, he was sold as a slave to Potiphar, an officer for pharaoh, the king. He was a kind man and treated Joseph well. Joseph worked faithfully for Potiphar, careful to do more than Potiphar expected him to do.

Potiphar was pleased with Joseph and gave him better work. One day he put him in charge of his entire household. No one was more important then than Joseph, except Potiphar and his family. Potiphar could see that Joseph was faithful to God and that God was with Joseph.

But Potiphar's wife fell in love with Joseph. She wanted Joseph to pretend that he was her husband. Joseph would not do that. He knew that he must be faithful to his master Potiphar. If he did what Potiphar's wife wanted, he could not be trusted.

Potiphar's wife was angry when Joseph turned away from her. She made up a story and told it to her husband, accusing Joseph of doing what she had wanted him to do. Potiphar believed his wife and angrily had Joseph thrown into prison.

Joseph could have blamed God for letting this happen. He could have pouted and sulked, but he didn't. Instead, he was faithful to the warden, the man in charge of the prison and did even more than he expected. The warden saw that Joseph could be trusted with anything and put him in charge of the other prisoners.

While Joseph was in prison, two of pharaoh's officers were put there also. One night pharaoh's cupbearer, one of the men, dreamed that he squeezed grapes into a cup and gave the cup to pharaoh. The other man, pharaoh's baker, dreamed that birds ate bread from baskets on his head.

"Your dream means that you will go back to work for pharaoh," Joseph told the cupbearer. "Remember me when you do."

"But your dream means that pharaoh will put you to death," Joseph told the baker.

On the third day after that, pharaoh had a birthday party. He gave a feast for his officers and brought his cupbearer back to work. But he had his baker put to death, just as Joseph had said.

The cupbearer forgot about Joseph, his companion in prison. But Joseph, even though he remained in prison, was faithful in all that he did.

## LEARN

From the story, you learn that peole apprcciatc a faithful person, even though some may forget about that faithfulness for a short time.

## DO

Look up the following Bible verses. They tell about the kind of faithfulness that Joseph had: Psalm 31:23; Proverbs 13:17; Matthew 25:21; 1 Timothy 1:12.

## THINK

1. How was Joseph faithful to Potiphar? How did Potiphar reward Joseph for his faithfulness? 2. How was Joseph faithful in prison? How did the warden reward Joseph? 3. How did the cupbearer forget about Joseph and his faithful work? How can you be faithful in your home and school?

29

# Joseph Becomes Governor

## A Story about HUMILITY

Days and weeks passed and Joseph was still in prison. He must have wondered if he would ever get out. He had been faithful to God, but that didn't seem to matter, for nothing happened to take him from prison or from being a slave. During all this time, though, Joseph kept humble before God. He never doubted and always seemed to put God first.

One night pharaoh, king of Egypt, had two strange dreams. When he woke up the dreams still disturbed him, so he sent for his magicians. But they could not tell him what the dreams meant.

Then pharaoh's cupbearer remembered Joseph. He told pharaoh how Joseph had known the meaning of his dream about the grapes.

Pharaoh quickly sent for Joseph. He told Joseph about his dreams. In one dream seven lean cows ate seven fat cows. In the other, seven withered heads of grain ate seven good head of grain.

"I hear that you can tell what dreams mean," said pharaoh.

Joseph could have taken all the credit. He could have bragged to pharaoh about how good he was at telling the meaning of dreams. But he didn't. Joseph always gave God the credit for such things. He was truly a humble man.

"I can't tell the meaning of dreams, but God can," said Joseph. "There are seven years of good crops in Egypt now. But after they have ended, there will be seven years of famine. Look for a wise man and put him in charge of the land. Have him collect a fifth of all the harvest and store it for the time of famine."

Pharaoh and his officers liked this plan. "Who is better for the job than you?" pharaoh said to Joseph. "The spirit of God is with you."

That day pharaoh made Joseph governor of Egypt. He gave Joseph the king's official signet ring, the one used to mark in wax on important papers showing they came from the king. He gave Joseph fine clothes, a beautiful wife from an important family, and one of the best chariots in the land.

Joseph came before pharaoh that day a slave and a prisoner. He left as governor of all Egypt.

But Joseph remained humble before God. Even as governor, he did not pretend that he was more important than God. And he asked God to be with him as he built granaries and stored grain that would keep Egypt, and his family, from starving.

## THINK

1. What did pharaoh ask Joseph to do for him? Why didn't Joseph say he could tell what dreams meant? 2. How did Joseph show that he was humble? 3. In what ways can you be humble or proud?

## LEARN

From this story, you learn that great people are often humble. Sometimes the greatest people are the most humble.

## DO

Look up Matthew 23:12. It tells what happened to Joseph, who humbled himself and was exalted as governor of Egypt. Would you like to memorize this verse?

# Joseph Forgives His Brothers

*A Story about* FORGIVENESS

"Where are you from?" the governor of Egypt demanded. The visitors bowed down before him with their faces to the ground. How could they know that this tall powerful man was their brother Joseph, the one they had sold as a slave years before? As they bowed, Joseph remembered his dream as a teenager, when his brothers' sheaves of grain bowed down to his.

"We are from Canaan," the brothers answered. "We have come to buy food."

"You are spies," Joseph shouted. "You want to find where our land is weak." Joseph was about to put his brothers through some hard tests. He must have wanted to reach out to them, to tell them who he was. But he must first learn if they were sorry for what they had done.

"We are twelve brothers," they said "Our youngest brother is home with our father. The other is dead."

"I will find out if you are telling the truth," said Joseph. "You must bring your younger brother here. If you don't, I will know that you are lying." Joseph had his brothers put into prison. They must learn what it was like to live in a dark, foul prison in Egypt.

After three days, Joseph took the brothers out again. "One of you must stay here in prison until the others return with your younger brother," he said. "Take grain back home to your hungry families, but your brother will not be set free until you return."

"We are being punished for what we did to Joseph," the brothers said to one another. They did not know that Joseph understood what they said, for he had been speaking through a man who knew both languages.

"I told you not to hurt Joseph," said Reuben. "But you wouldn't listen to me."

When Joseph heard what the brothers said, he turned away from them and wept. Now he had heard for the first time that they were truly sorry that they had sold him as a slave.

Joseph ordered Simeon to be bound while the other brothers watched. Then he quietly gave orders for his brothers' sacks to be filled with grain and their money put into their sacks. Of course, when the brothers opened their sacks later and found the money, they were afraid. "What is God doing to us?" they asked.

Jacob was disturbed when he heard what had happened to Simeon. He was even more disturbed to hear that the governor had demanded that Benjamin come to Egypt. If he did not, the brothers could not buy grain and Simeon would not go free.

Jacob refused to let Benjamin go, even though Reuben promised to be personally responsible and take special care of him.

Then the famine grew worse. The corn they had brought from Egypt was all gone and Jacob had to send his sons back to Egypt to buy more. But they were afraid and would not go unless Benjamin went with them. Now Judah also promised to guard him very carefully.

Finally Jacob agreed to let Benjamin go. He also sent a special gift to the governor, along with some fruit, honey, spices and nuts. He told the brothers to take twice as much money with them, and to return the money they had found in their sacks before.

When the brothers arrived in Egypt with Benjamin, Joseph ordered them to come to his house for dinner. They were even more afraid then, and they wondered what the governor would do to them. They thought he would accuse them of stealing the money and that he would make them prisoners.

On the way to Joseph's house, the brothers talked with the man in charge of Joseph's things. "We brought more money because we found our money in the sacks last time," they said.

"Don't worry about it," the man answered. "You paid for the grain. You owe us nothing."

Then he released Simeon from prison and brought him to his brothers.

When Joseph arrived at his house, the brothers were waiting with the gifts they had brought from Canaan. They bowed and he asked about their father. They bowed again and said he was well.

At dinner, Joseph seated the brothers by age. Think how surprised they were when they saw that! But they ate the good food and actually seemed to enjoy this unusual meal.

After dinner the sacks were filled and the men headed home. Of course they did not know that Joseph had had his silver cup hidden in Benjamin's sack. Joseph sent his steward to catch up with the men and when he found the silver cup, the brothers were sure they would all go to prison.

They were terrified as they stood before Joseph and his guard with the silver cup. Joseph told them the one in whose sack the cup had been found would have to be his servant. The rest of them could go home. He wanted to see if they were still jealous or if they really cared about what happened to Benjamin.

Judah quickly begged the governor to let him stay as the servant in Benjamin's place and to let his youngest brother go back to their father.

When he heard that, Joseph could keep

his secret no longer. He sent all the servants out of the room and when he was alone with his brothers, he cried out, "I am Joseph!" Then he began to weep. The brothers were so shocked and afraid they didn't know what to say.

Almost anyone in Joseph's place would have had those brothers punished for selling him as a slave. But not Joseph. "God sent me here to Egypt to save your lives," Joseph told them. Then he forgave them for the things they had done.

This beautiful story of forgiveness ends with Jacob and his entire family moving to Egypt. There Joseph cared for them as long as they lived. So everyone did live happily ever after, because the son who was sold as a slave forgave.

## THINK

1. What had Joseph's brothers done to him that was wrong? 2. How could Joseph have gotten even with them when they came to buy grain? Why didn't he? 3. How did he forgive them? How did the story end happily?

## LEARN

From this story, you learn that stories and lives end happily when people truly forgive.

## DO

Do you need to forgive someone for something that person has done to you? Forgiveness is only one letter or phone call away. Will you write the letter or make that phone call now…and forgive?

# God Takes Care of Baby Moses

*A Story about* PROVIDING

Many years had passed since Joseph's family had moved to Egypt. As the years went by, Joseph and his brothers died, and so did their children and their children's children. New pharaohs came and went too. For a while, the pharaohs remembered how Joseph had saved Egypt from famine and they treated his family well. But at last there came a pharaoh who did not care. He was afraid of these Hebrews, the people descended from Joseph and his brothers, because there were so many of them. "What if they side with our enemies and fight against us?" he wondered.

So this pharaoh put slave masters over the Hebrews and they forced the Hebrews to build cities for the Egyptians. Even so, the Hebrews grew in numbers faster than the Egyptians.

Pharaoh tried to force the Egyptian midwives, women who helped other women have babies, to kill the Hebrew boys as soon as they were born. But the midwives feared God and refused to do it.

At last pharaoh gave orders for every Hebrew baby boy to be thrown into the Nile River. Then he sent his soldiers to see that it was done.

Amram and Jochebed, a Hebrew slave couple, were afraid, for they had just had a new baby boy. If he were found, pharaoh's soldiers would throw him into the river. What could they do to protect him? For three months they tried one way and then another. At last they knew they would soon be discovered.

Then Jochebed had a plan. She wove a basket from the papyrus reeds that grew along the Nile River. She coated it with tar and pitch and hid the basket among the reeds in the shallow part of the river. Miriam, the baby's older sister, sat nearby to watch. Now they must have prayed that God would protect their baby.

One day pharaoh's daughter came to the river to bathe. As she and her attendants walked along the river they heard a baby crying. Pharaoh's daughter looked in the basket and saw the baby. She felt sorry for him and wanted to keep him. She would protect him from pharaoh's soldiers.

Miriam quickly appeared. "Shall I find a Hebrew nurse for you?" she asked.

"Yes," said pharaoh's daughter. Of course Miriam brought her mother.

Pharaoh's daughter named the baby Moses and left him in his mother's care. God had protected Moses in a special way. Moses would be safe now, safe to grow up to serve God, who had taken care of him.

## THINK

1. What did Jochebed do to protect Moses? 2. What did Miriam do? 3. How did pharaoh's daughter protect Moses? 4. What do you think God did in all this to protect Moses? 5. Think of some ways God protects you. What are they?

## LEARN

From this story, you learn that God protects in wonderful ways.

## DO

On a sheet of paper, or a card, write down five things you think could hurt you. Now pray that god will protect you from them.

# Moses at the Burning Bush

*A Story about* OBEDIENCE

Moses often thought of that day in Egypt when he had killed an Egyptian guard. But what else could he have done? The guard was torturing a Hebrew slave and Moses could not let that happen.

Yet because of that, Moses had to run away from Egypt and hide in Midian. Now he was a shepherd, taking care of his father-in-law's sheep in the wilderness near Mount Sinai.

While Moses was watching the sheep one day, he was startled to see a bush burning, but not burning up. He moved closer and closer to see what was happening. Suddenly a voice called from the bush, "Moses! Moses!"

Moses was afraid. "Here I am," he answered.

"Take off your sandals," the voice called. "The place where you stand is holy ground. I am the God of your father, the God of Abraham, Isaac, and Jacob."

When Moses heard that, he hid his face. He was afraid to look at God, for it was said that to look at God would cause death.

"I have seen the suffering of my people in Egypt," God said. "I will rescue them. You must go back to Egypt to lead them out of their slavery."

Moses was afraid to go back to Egypt, so he began to make excuses, but it was no use. God had chosen him to lead his people from Egypt. Moses must go. He knew he would suffer and face much trouble. But when God says go, why should anyone say no? So Moses obeyed God and went back to Egypt. Wouldn't you?

## THINK

1. Why did Moses not want to go back to Egypt? 2. What did God want him to do there? 3. Why did Moses obey God? 4. Why should you obey God?

## LEARN

From this story, you learn that you should obey God.

## DO

Draw a big O on a piece of paper. Now put a B lying across the inside to form eyes, add an E lying across where the mouth should go and add a small Y for the nose. You have a little face to put on your wall to remind you to OBEY.

# The Ten Plagues

*A Story about* POWER

Who is more powerful, the God of Moses and his people or the gods of the Egyptians? Pharaoh thought his gods were more powerful. But Moses knew that God was greater.

For many years, pharaoh had kept Moses' people, the Hebrews, in slavery. He had made them work hard, building cities for him. Of course pharaoh did not pay them. He gave them only enough food to keep them strong for his work, and a tiny hut to live in.

God did not want His people to be slaves. Moses did not want his people to be slaves either. But as long as pharaoh thought his gods were greater than Moses' god, he would not let these people go free.

That is why God spoke to Moses in a special way and sent him back to Egypt. God wanted Moses to tell pharaoh to let the people go. And God chose Moses' brother Aaron to help him.

"God says you must let my people go free," Moses told pharaoh. But pharaoh was angry. He would not give up all that free work.

"Who is your God, and why should I do what He says?" pharaoh asked. "Show me how powerful He is."

Aaron threw down his shepherd's rod and it became a snake. Surely no one else could do that. But pharaoh's magicians had some strange power. When they threw down their rods, they became snakes too. You can imagine how surprised Moses and Aaron were to see that! But God showed He was more powerful than the Egyptian gods. Aaron's snake ate up all the other snakes! It didn't convince pharaoh, though. He still thought his gods were as powerful as the God of Moses and his people.

On the next visit, Moses and Aaron caused the first of the ten plagues to come to the land of Egypt. Each of them became more terrible than the one before. The first was the plague of blood, when Moses touched the Nile River and the water turned to blood. Somehow, pharaoh's magicians could do this too. So pharaoh still didn't think the God of Moses was more powerful than the gods of Egypt.

Moses and Aaron came back to pharaoh to bring another plague. This time they caused frogs to come up on the land by the thousands. But pharaoh's magicians could do this too. So pharaoh still thought his gods were as powerful as the God of Moses and his people.

The next time Moses and Aaron came to pharaoh, they caused a plague of lice or gnats to go on all the animals of Egypt. Pharaoh's magicians could not do this. Now the magicians began to see how much power God had. But pharaoh's heart was hard and he wouldn't listen to them.

Swarms of flies came next. This time Moses told pharaoh that God would divide the people and the flies would only come upon the Egyptians. God would not let them come to His people. After God sent the flies, pharaoh said the people should worship their God but they could not go free.

The next plague God sent caused the cattle, the horses, and many other animals to become sick and die. Now pharaoh and his people began to be afraid, for they worshiped the cow and bull. God was showing that He was stronger than the cow god, Hathor, or the bull god, Apis.

Another plague made painful boils break out upon all the Egyptian people and on the animals that were left. Many of the Egyptian people began to believe that the God of Moses was the most powerful. But pharaoh's heart just got harder, and he would not admit it. He still would not let the people go.

When hail came and destroyed most of the crops of Egypt, that showed that God was greater than all the Egyptian gods of the harvest. Now pharaoh sent for Moses and Aaron. He told them he was wrong. If they would stop the hail, he would let the people go. When Moses and Aaron stopped the hail, though, pharaoh changed his mind. He would not let the people of Israel go free.

When locusts came and destroyed the rest of the crops of Egypt, he did the same thing again.

One day darkness came across the land. It was so thick they could feel it and their lamps wouldn't make any light. But it came only to the Egyptians. God's people, the children of Israel, had light in their homes. The Egyptians thought their greatest god of all, Re, the god of the sun, had died in his nightly journey under the earth. They thought he fought a great snake each night and if the snake ever won, the sun would not shine again. So when the sun did not shine for three days, they were sure their greatest god had lost.

Then a plague worse than darkness came. All the firstborn animals and people died, even pharaoh's oldest son. It was clear now that God controlled life and death. Now pharaoh and his people feared Moses' God, for they thought much about life and death, and feared for their own lives.

At last the contest was over. Moses' God was more powerful than all the gods of Egypt. The magicians, the Egyptian people, and even pharaoh, all knew that now.

## THINK

1. How do you know that God is more powerful than all the gods of Egypt? 2. Why do you think He is more powerful than anyone else today?

## LEARN

From this story, you learn that God is more powerful than anyone else, even the gods of Egypt.

## DO

Draw a picture of the three most powerful things you can think of. Think of such things as the sun, a volcano, and storm clouds. Which of these does God control?

# The Exodus from Egypt

## *A Story about* OBEDIENCE

"Tell your people to do exactly what I say," the Lord said to Moses. Moses listened carefully. The people listened carefully too when Moses told them what the Lord said.

The Lord told the people how to prepare a special meal, called the Passover. He told them what meat to use, how to eat it, and how to sprinkle the lamb's blood on the doorposts of their homes.

"I will pass through Egypt and will strike every firstborn man and animal," the Lord warned. "When I see the blood on a doorpost, I will pass over you."

The Hebrews did exactly what the Lord said. But of course the Egyptians did not. That night the angel of death passed through Egypt. All firstborn men and animals died, except in houses with the blood on the doorposts.

The people of Egypt were terrified. There was hardly a home in Egypt where the angel of death had not touched some relative. Now the Egyptians were pleading for the Hebrews to leave. They were so anxious that they gave jewelry and gold and precious gifts to get them on their way.

At last pharaoh called for Moses and Aaron. "Go! Get out of the land!" he urged.

The people of Israel, the Hebrews, were free! What a procession they made as they left the city and went their way through the wilderness toward the Promised Land. They were safe and they were free because they had obeyed the Lord completely.

## THINK

1. What do you think would have happened if the people had not obeyed the Lord completely? 2. What happened to the Hebrews, the people of Israel, because they did obey? 3. Why should you obey the Lord? 4. Why should you obey your parents?

## LEARN

From this story, you learn that good things happen to those who obey the Lord.

## DO

Tell this story again, but pretend that Moses' people refused to obey the Lord. How would the story go on from there?

# Crossing the Red Sea

## *A Story about* TRUST

"What have we done?" pharaoh began to wonder. "We have let all those slaves go free and have lost their work."

Pharaoh had begun to see how much work the Hebrews had done. Now that they were gone, who was there to do this work? He began to see how much work would not get done without them.

Pharaoh ordered men to get his chariot and prepare his army for battle. He had heard how the Hebrews were moving about in the wilderness and thought they must surely not know where they were going. His spies must have told him how the Israelites were trapped at a camp by the sea and how easy it would be to conquer them there.

So pharaoh's chariots, horsemen, and troops pursued as quickly as they could and found the Israelites trapped by the sea. Moses knew why they were there, of course, for the Lord had told him. But the people of Israel did not know. They were terrified to see pharaoh and his chariots and horsemen approaching. They were sure that they could not escape for they did not trust the Lord to save them. Some began to complain to Moses.

"Why have you brought us out here to die?" they said. "Didn't we tell you to leave us in Egypt? It would be better to serve the Egyptians there than die out here."

"Don't be afraid," said Moses. "Trust the Lord and see how He will deliver you. The Lord will fight for you."

As evening came, the Lord moved the cloud that led the Israelites until it was between them and the Egyptians. The Egyptian army had to stop, for they could not see where they were going.

At the Lord's command, Moses stretched out his rod and his hand across the sea. All night the Lord drove the sea apart with a strong wind and made a path across the sea on dry land. When morning came, Moses led his people to the other side of the sea, with a wall of water on each side of them. Moses and his people trusted God to keep the water there until they had crossed.

At the right moment, the Lord took His cloud away, and the Egyptian army pursued. But when they reached the sea, the Lord let the waters rush back upon them and they were drowned.

Now the people of Israel saw how the Lord could do great miracles to save His people. They knew that they had not trusted Him

fully. It was an important lesson for them to learn, one they would have to learn again and again in the wilderness.

## THINK

1. Why did pharaoh go after the people of Israel? 2. How did the people of Israel fail to trust the Lord to take care of them? 3. How did they learn that they could trust the Lord and He would take care of them? 4. What did you learn about trusting the Lord?

## LEARN

From this story, you learn that you can trust the Lord and He will take care of you.

## DO

Psalm 56:3,4 are good verses to memorize. So are Proverbs 3:5,6. Would you like to memorize one pair of these now?

# Israel in the Wilderness

## A Story about PROVIDING

There were no grocery stores in the wilderness, no wells, no gardens or vineyards, and no rivers where the people could fish. The people had never lived in the wilderness before, so they began to worry about food and water. All that first day in the wilderness they marched over the hot sands but found no food or water. The second day was just like the first. By this time the people were getting frantic. Then the third day came. Still no food or water. The situation looked desperate! At last they came to a spring. They could hardly wait to drink. Imagine how disappointed they were to find that the water was bitter.

Moses cried to the Lord and the Lord showed him some wood. When he put it into the water, it became sweet and the people could drink it.

Step by step through the wilderness it was this way. At one place, the Lord led the people to some springs with palm trees around them. At another place he showed Moses how to strike a rock to get water. But always there was enough water, for the Lord provided.

There was also the problem of food. The Lord provided that, too. Each day He sent little flakes of food called manna. There was always enough. The Israelites did not starve in the wilderness, for the Lord was with them. He always provided enough for each day.

## THINK

1. Did any of the Israelites starve to death or die of thirst in the wilderness?   2. Who took care of them and provided food and water?   3. Has the Lord provided enough food and water for you each day?

## LEARN

From this story, you learn that God does provide, giving you enough food and water for each day.

## DO

Draw some of the different places where God provides water for you. Don't forget a faucet, a drinking fountain, a pump, and a stream. Can you think of others?

# The Ten Commandments

*A Story about* OBEDIENCE

Most people don't like to obey orders. They like to do what they want to do, not what someone else tells them. But the Lord knew that people could not live that way. Things would get too confusing.

When the people of Israel reached Mount Sinai, the Lord told Moses to set up camp. He and the Israelites would stay there for quite some time. They would build a tent where they could worship the Lord, and He would give them His laws through Moses.

The Lord gave Moses many laws for the people to follow. But ten of them seemed more important than the others. Perhaps that is because the Lord thought they were so important that He wrote them Himself, with His own finger, on tablets of stone. Then He gave them to Moses on the top of Mount Sinai.

Today people still try to follow these ten laws, called The Ten Commandments. Do you know them? This is what they say: 1. Do not worship any other gods instead of Me. 2. Do not make idols or worship them. 3. Do not use the Lord's name in the wrong way. 4. Honor the Lord on the seventh day. 5. Honor your father and mother. 6. Do not murder. 7. Do not pretend someone else's husband or wife is yours. 8. Do not steal. 9. Do not lie. 10. Do not want what belongs to someone else.

These are all good laws, aren't they? They are even good enough for us to remember and obey today.

## THINK

1. How important are The Ten Commandments? 2. Do you try to do what they say? 3. Jesus said that following The Ten Commandments is not enough to get us to heaven. We must accept Him to do that. But they are important for us to follow, so that we can please Him.

## LEARN

From this story, you learn that God's rules are good rules and help us please Him.

## DO

Have you ever memorized The Ten Commandments? It's hard to do if you learn the entire Bible section. But you can memorize the short statements in this story. Would you like to do that?

# Twelve Spies Visit Canaan

*A Story about* TRUST

"Send some men to explore the land," the Lord told Moses. The land was The Promised Land, which the Lord promised to give to Moses and his people. But they would have to go in and take it.

Moses chose one man from each of the twelve tribes. Then he sent them into The Promised Land to explore.

"What kind of land is it? Is it good or bad? What kind of towns do the people live in? Do the towns have walls and forts? Is the soil good or poor? Are there trees? What kinds of fruits grow there?" These were questions the spies were to answer.

So the twelve spies went into The Promised Land. They went through the land, from one end to the other. On their way back, they stopped in the Valley of Eshcol and cut a large bunch of grapes. It was so large that two men had to carry it on a pole. They also carried pomegranates and figs.

When the spies returned, they gave their report to Moses and the leaders. "The land is rich, but the people are powerful," they said. "They live in large cities with walls and forts. Some of the people are giants."

One of the twelve spies, Caleb, asked the people to be quiet while he spoke. "We should go into this land and take possession," said Caleb. "We can do it!" Caleb trusted the Lord to help them win.

But ten of the spies did not trust the Lord to help them win.

"The men are too powerful," they argued. "We looked like grasshoppers beside them."

That night the people of Israel grumbled against Moses and Aaron. They talked about getting new leaders and going back to Egypt. Then Moses and Aaron fell on their faces before the Lord in front of all the people, begging the Lord for His help.

Joshua, one of the spies, urged the people to go into the land and take it. "Don't rebel against the Lord," he said. "The Lord is with us." Like Caleb, Joshua showed that he trusted the Lord to help them.

But the people refused to listen. They even talked about stoning Moses and Aaron. Then the Lord appeared at the tabernacle and spoke. "Not one person who rebelled against Me and failed to trust Me will go into The Promised Land," He said. "Every grownup will die in the wilderness except Joshua and Caleb. Then, when your children grow up, they will be able to go into The Promised Land." When the people heard that, they were sorry that they had not trusted the Lord, but it was too late now.

## THINK

1. What great miracles had the Lord done for these people since they left Egypt? Why should those miracles have shown them that they could trust the Lord for help? 2. Why should your trust the Lord to help you each day?

## LEARN

From this story, you learn that the Lord will do great and wonderful things if we trust Him.

## DO

Do you remember the bunch of grapes the people brought back? Draw a bunch of grapes like that on some paper. Put one of these letters in each grape: T R U S T. What should that help you remember to do?

# Rahab Helps Two Spies

## A Story about KINDNESS

"Go into The Promised Land and find out what you can," Joshua told two spies. "Look especially at Jericho."

The people of Israel were ready to go into The Promised Land to live. But they must first fight the people who lived there, and conquer them. If they didn't, they would be driven back into the wilderness or would all be killed.

The two spies crossed the Jordan River and went to Jericho. That was the first city the Israelites must conquer. The spies must learn whatever they could to help their people win in a battle.

The spies stayed at a house built on Jericho's wall. The owner, a woman named Rahab, rented rooms to travelers. But someone saw the men come into Jericho and told the king. The king sent men to capture them.

When Rahab heard that the king's men were coming, she hid the spies under some flax on her rooftop. Then she told the king's men, "They were here, but they left just before sunset in time to get outside the city gate. Hurry, and you may catch them."

As soon as the king's men left, Rahab went up to the rooftop to have a talk with the spies. "I know that the Lord has already given this land to you," she said. "Our people are afraid of you because of the miracles which the Lord has done for you. I have shown kindness to you by keeping you safe, so please show kindness to me and my family when you conquer Jericho."

"You have been kind and saved our lives, so we will be kind and save yours," the spies said. "But you must tie this scarlet cord in your window. When we come to conquer, whoever is in the house will be saved. Whoever is outside the house will be killed."

Rahab agreed, and tied the scarlet cord in her window. It would remind the men and their army of Rahab's kindness, and of their promise to be kind to her.

## THINK

1. How was Rahab kind to the two spies? Why did she do this? 2. How did Rahab want the spies and their army to be kind to her? 3. How would the Israelite army know Rahab's house? 4. How has the Lord been kind to you? 5. What can you do to say thank you and show kindness in return?

## LEARN

From this story, you learn that one kindness deserves another. When someone is kind to you, be kind to that person also.

## DO

Ask your mother to help you find a red string, piece of yarn, or thread, and hang it in your window this week. Each time you see it, remember to be kind to others, especially to your family.

# Crossing the Jordan River

## A Story about DEDICATION

For the last 40 years the people of Israel had traveled through the wilderness, headed for The Promised Land. They dreamed of the day when they would get there, settle down, build their homes, and plant their gardens and vineyards. Most of the people who started on this long trip had died in the wilderness, but their children had grown up and had come at last to the Jordan River. As soon as they crossed the river, they would be in the land that the Lord had promised them.

On the night before they crossed the river, Joshua spoke to the people. "Dedicate yourselves to the Lord," Joshua told the people. "Tomorrow the Lord will do amazing things for you."

The people dedicated themselves to the Lord. They promised to do exactly what He said.

The next day, Joshua told the people how the Lord wanted them to cross the river. Because the people had dedicated themselves to the Lord, they did exactly what the Lord told them through Joshua.

"Carry the ark of the covenant into the river," Joshua told the priests. They did exactly what Joshua said. When they stepped into the river, the water stopped so the priests walked out to the middle of the riverbed on dry ground. Then the people crossed to the other side without getting their feet wet.

"Come up out of the riverbed, to the other side," Joshua told the priest who carried the ark. When they did exactly what Joshua said, the water filled the river again. The people were all safe now in The Promised Land.

"Put twelve stones into a pile," Joshua ordered. "They will help you remember what the Lord has done today." They did exactly what the Lord said through Joshua. They were glad, too, for the stones reminded them often how the Lord had helped them go into the land He had promised.

## THINK

1. When the people dedicated themselves to the Lord, what did they promise to do? 2. How did they keep their promise? 3. What did they do to remind them of all that the Lord had done that day?

## LEARN

From this story, you learn that when you dedicate yourself to the Lord, you do exactly what He wants. This is good to remember, isn't it?

## DO

It is good to have something nearby to remind us of the Lord. Your Bible lying in your room reminds you to read it. A motto, or Bible verse, on your wall reminds you to pray or please the Lord some other way. Some people put pictures of missionaries on their wall to remember to pray for them. Put up something today to remind you to do something the Lord wants you to do.

# Joshua Captures Jericho

## A Story about OBEDIENCE

"Obey Me and Jericho will be yours," the Lord said to Joshua. Joshua listened carefully. He remembered what had happened before. Whenever the people of Israel obeyed the Lord, He helped them. When they did not obey Him, they got into trouble.

Joshua called his people together. Then he told them what the Lord had said. "Obey the Lord and He will help us capture the city," Joshua said.

Joshua's soldiers should have been afraid. Jericho had great walls and mighty warriors. How could they hope to get into the city to fight? How could they get over those walls?

But Joshua's soldiers were not afraid. Instead, the people of Jericho were afraid. They had heard how the Lord had helped the people of Israel on the way to The Promised Land.

"March around Jericho six days," Joshua commanded. Seven priests went first, blowing their trumpets, followed by more priests who carried the ark of the covenant. An armed guard went before the trumpeters, and another armed guard followed the ark. Israel's fighting men followed.

Each day for six days the Israelites marched around Jericho once. On the seventh day they marched around the city seven times. Then Joshua commanded, "Shout, for the Lord has given you the city."

The people shouted and Jericho's walls came tumbling down. The people of Israel had done exactly what the Lord said. The city of Jericho was theirs.

---

### THINK

1. What did the Lord tell the Israelites to do to conquer Jericho? 2. What did the Israelites do? 3. What might have been different if they had not obeyed the Lord completely?

---

### LEARN

From this story, you learn that it is important to obey the Lord.

---

### DO

Who should you obey? What about your parents? What about the Lord? Draw a smiling face on a card. That will help you remember to obey your parents. Draw a rectangle and write Bible on it. That will help you remember to obey the Lord, and to do what He says in His Word. Keep these in a place where you will see them often.

# Gideon's 300

## A Story about COURAGE

"You have too many soldiers," the Lord told Gideon. Gideon was surprised. How can an army have too many soldiers, especially when it is going to fight a much larger army?

Gideon was going out to fight the Midianites, a tribe of people who had been stealing the Israelite crops and leaving the people hungry. Once and for all he and his men must defeat these enemies or the Israelites would starve.

"If you win the battle with that many men, you will think your army did it without My help and will brag about it," the Lord said. "Send home the men who are afraid."

When Gideon told his army what the Lord said, 22,000 men went home. They did not have the courage to fight. There were only 10,000 left. "There are still too many," the Lord said. Then the Lord told Gideon how to keep only the very best. Gideon did exactly what the Lord said. He led his men down to a stream and told them to drink. Those who bent down and lapped the water like animals were sent home. They were not careful soldiers, for they could not see while they were drinking. Those who scooped water into their hands and looked around while they drank were kept. But there were only 300 of them. Those men had to have the courage to stay and fight with Gideon.

Gideon and his 300 listened carefully to the Lord. He told them what to do. In the middle of the night, they went up to a hill surrounding the enemy camp with trumpets, torches, and clay pitchers. They covered their torches with the pitchers and at a signal from Gideon, broke the pitchers, blew on the trumpets, and shouted. The enemy soldiers were completely surprised and thought they were outnumbered, so they began to fight each other. Each thought the others were Gideon's soldiers.

The 300 soldiers of Gideon could never brag that they had won the battle. The Lord had told them what to do. He had been with them and had helped them defeat a great army.

How did these men have so much courage? Because they trusted the Lord, they could do things the way He said. That's a good rule for us to remember, too.

## THINK

1. Why did the Lord say Gideon had too many soldiers? 2. How did the Lord help Gideon send 32,000 men home? 3. Why do you think Gideon and his 300 men had courage?

## LEARN

From this story you learn that you have courage to do what you should when you trust the Lord to help you.

## DO

Are you afraid of something or someone? Who can help you? Why not ask Him to help you now?

# Samson Marries a Philistine

## A Story about SELF-CONTROL

"I want to marry this girl," Samson insisted. Samson's parents could not believe that Samson wanted to marry a Philistine. At this time the Philistines ruled Israel, and the two nations were bitter enemies.

But Samson would not listen to his parents. "Can't you find a wife among our own people?" Samson's parents asked. But Samson would not listen to them. He would do what he wanted to do.

So Samson set out for the Philistine town of Timnah with his mother and father. While his parents were making wedding arrangements, Samson walked alone in a vineyard. Suddenly a fierce young lion leaped at him from the bushes. Samson easily wrestled the lion to the ground and killed it, for the Lord had made Samson the strongest man in Israel.

Soon it was Samson's wedding day and he returned to Timnah. On the way he stopped to look at the young lion he had killed. A swarm of bees had made a nest in the body of the lion and Samson ate some honey.

Samson arrived at the wedding feast and made a deal with the Philistine men there. "If you can guess my riddle in seven days" he said, "I will give each of you two coats. But if you do not guess the riddle, you must each give me two coats." The men agreed and Samson told them this riddle about the lion, "From the eater came something to eat. From the strong came something sweet."

The Philistine men could not guess the riddle. So they went to Samson's wife and said they would kill her if she did not get the answer for them. She nagged Samson so much that finally on the last day, Samson could not control himself and told her the answer. The men then came to Samson and said, "What is sweeter than honey, or stronger than a lion?"

Samson was angry that he had not controlled his tongue and kept the answer a secret. He marched in a rage to the city of Ashkelon, killed thirty Philistine men there, and took their coats to the men at the wedding feast. Then he went home to his parents and left his wife behind.

Samson certainly knew that he had disappointed the Lord. Instead of putting his thoughts and actions under the Lord's control, he did what he wanted.

## THINK

1. Who did Samson want to please, the Lord, or himself? 2. How did Samson fail to control his mind and body? 3. Why does the Lord want you to keep control of yourself? How does that please Him?

## LEARN

From this story, you learn that you please the Lord by keeping control of yourself.

## DO

Memorize Galatians 5:22. The next time you think you are not pleasing the Lord, say the verse to yourself. What should that help you do?

# Samson and Delilah

## *A Story about* FAITHFULNESS

Would you like to be the strongest person in the world? Samson was. Because he was so strong, all Israel hoped that Samson would lead them. That is what the Lord wanted too. But Samson was not a good leader because he did not use his strength to please the Lord.

One time Samson spent the night with a Philistine woman in Gaza. Samson knew this was wrong and would not please the Lord. But he did it anyway. The men of Gaza planned to kill him at dawn. They were afraid that Samson might hurt them. So the Philistines surrounded the city and locked the heavy city gate.

But Samson learned of the plot. He got up in the middle of the night, grabbed the wooden doors of the gate, and tore the entire gate from the ground. Then he carried it to the top of a hill far away.

Some time later, Samson fell in love with a Philistine woman named Delilah. When the Philistine rulers found out they told Delilah, "If you can find the secret to Samson's strength, we will make you rich."

One day Delilah said to Samson, "Tell me the secret of your great strength. Can anything take it away?"

"If anyone ties me with seven fresh bowstrings, I will be as weak as any other man," Samson lied. That night when Samson fell asleep, Delilah tied Samson's arms and legs with seven fresh bowstrings. Philistine soldiers were hiding in the other room. "Samson, get up! The Philistines are after you," she shouted. Samson jumped up and snapped the bowstrings as if they were not there.

Again and again Delilah tried to learn the secret of Samson's strength. And each time Samson tricked her by making up a story about the source of his strength. But Delilah nagged him so much that at last he gave in. He foolishly told her the truth. "Long ago I made a vow to god that I would not cut my hair. If I do, I will become as weak as any other man."

That night Samson again fell asleep on Delilah's lap, and she shaved the hair from his head. "Samson, the Philistines are after you!" she shouted. Samson jumped up, but this time his strength was gone. He had broken his promise to God. The Philistines seized him and gouged out his eyes. Then they led him away in chains to prison.

The Lord gave Samson the ability to become a great man. But Samson wasted his

time and ability on the wrong people. Samson learned the hard way that it is better to use your strength for the Lord than for yourself.

## THINK

1. Who was the strongest man in the world? 2. Who gave him this strength? 3. Did Samson use his strength to please the Lord or to please himself? 4. How should you use your strength?

## LEARN

From this story, you learn that you should use your strength to please the Lord.

## DO

What do you do best? Do you play an instrument best? Do you play ball best? Or do you do you best in school work? The next time you do what you do best, tell the Lord you are doing it for Him.

67

# The Story of Ruth

## A Story about LOVE

The rain did not fall and the crops did not grow in Israel for a long time. Some people had to move away because there was no food. One family, Elimelech, Naomi, and their two sons, moved to Moab where the sons married Moabite girls, Ruth and Orpah. As time passed, Elimelech and his two sons died, leaving Naomi alone with these two girls.

One day Naomi decided to return to Israel where many of her people still worshiped God. The people in Moab did not do that. Orpah decided to stay in Moab with her friends, but Ruth went with Naomi. Together the two walked many miles to Bethlehem where Naomi once lived.

Ruth loved Naomi and tried to make her happy. Each day during harvest time Ruth went to the fields which a man named Boaz owned. There she followed the men who cut the stalks of grain and tied them into bundles. She picked up stalks of grain they had left behind and beat the grain from it.

"Who is that young woman?" Boaz asked his men one day. "That is Ruth," the men said. "She is the one who came from Moab with Naomi." Boaz wanted to talk with Ruth. "I have heard that you have been good to your mother-in-law Naomi," Boaz told her. "God will bless you for that." Then Boaz asked Ruth to come to his field each day to pick up grain. "I will take care of you," he said.

Ruth worked faithfully in the fields, and each day brought grain home to Naomi. Boaz began to love Ruth and soon asked her to marry him. Together, Ruth and Boaz took care of Naomi.

God blessed Ruth because she was kind to Naomi, and because she had chosen God as her God. And God was happy that Ruth, Boaz and Naomi loved each other.

## THINK

1. How do you know that Ruth loved Naomi? What did Ruth do for her? 2. Who fell in love with Ruth? What did Boaz and Ruth do for Naomi? Why do you think they did this? 3. When you love someone, what will you do for them?

## LEARN

From this story, you learn that you do good things for those you love.

## DO

How much do you love your parents? Would you like to do something good for them? Write something you would like to do on a card. For example: GOOD FOR WASHING DISHES TONIGHT. Then give it to the parent whom it will help most. Be sure to do what you say.

# Samuel—a Boy Who Honored God

## A Story about REVERENCE

Someone called Samuel's name! Samuel sat up in bed and looked around his big tent home. He saw nothing but shadows from the flickering yellow light of the oil lamps. The shadows danced upon the golden chest across the room. They played upon the angel-like figures that stood with outstretched wings upon this chest.

The big tent where Samuel lived was God's house. Many years ago Moses and his people had made it in the wilderness. They had carried it here to Shiloh when they came into the Promised Land. Now the boy Samuel lived here and helped the old priest Eli take care of God's house. Eli was glad, for Samuel showed reverence, or honor, for God and Eli's sons did not. So Samuel slept in one of the most important places in God's house, near the golden chest, the Ark of the Covenant. Here he heard God call his name.

"Samuel! Samuel!" God's voice called. Samuel thought Eli was calling. He jumped from his bed and ran to ask Eli what he wanted.

"I did not call you," Eli told Samuel. "Go back to bed."

Samuel went back to bed but soon he heard God's voice calling his name. Again Samuel ran to ask Eli what he wanted.

"I did not call you!" Eli told Samuel. "Go back to bed!"

Once more Samuel heard God's voice calling. Once more he ran to ask Eli what he wanted.

Now Eli knew that God was calling Samuel. He told Samuel that God must have something important to tell him.

"Go back to bed," Eli told Samuel. "When you hear God's voice again, tell Him that you are listening."

When God spoke this time, Samuel listened carefully. "Eli's sons do not honor Me or reverence Me," God told Samuel. "I have warned Eli and his sons, but Eli does nothing to stop them. Now I will punish them."

When morning came, Eli made Samuel tell him what God said. Of course Eli was sad. But he knew that these things were true.

"Let God do what He knows is best," Eli whispered.

As time passed, people all over the land saw that Samuel honored God in all that he did. They saw also that God was with Samuel.

## THINK

1. Think about the things God said about Eli's sons. Would you want God to say these things about you? 2. Now think about Samuel, and the way God helped him. Would you rather have God do this for you?

## LEARN

From this story, you learn that you should show REVERENCE, or honor, to God.

## DO

Find, or draw, a picture of a church, a Bible, and some people your age. Put these pictures in your room to remind you this week to honor, or reverence, God by going to His house, reading His Word, and telling your friends about Him.

# Israel's First King

## A Story about DECISION

"God has chosen you to be Israel's first king," Samuel said to Saul. Saul was surprised. He was a farmer, not a king. Only a few days ago he had left his father's home to search for some runaway donkeys. Someone thought the prophet Samuel could help him find the donkeys, so he came here to Samuel to ask. Now Samuel was telling Saul that he would be the next king of Israel!

Samuel took a jar of perfumed olive oil and poured it over Saul's head. This was called anointing. It showed that God wanted the man to be king. "Let God be with you," Samuel said. "Do whatever you decide is best, and He will not fail you."

Sometime later Samuel told the people of Israel to gather at Mizpeh. "You asked for a king," he said to them. "Now God has chosen a man named Saul to be your king." When Saul stood before the people, he was taller than anyone else in Israel. He certainly looked like he would make a good king. But would he be ready when the people needed him?

It wasn't long before the people did need him. A wicked king surrounded Jabesh, a city in Israel. "Let me gouge out every man's right eye," the king declared. "If you do not,

I will destroy your city."

"Give us seven days to decide," replied the men of Jabesh. They sent messengers to Saul to tell him about their trouble. Saul remembered Samuel's words. He decided that he must fight this king. Quickly Saul gathered soldiers and during the night defeated the wicked king and his men.

The people were glad that day that Saul was their king. Saul knew that as long as he was close to God, God would help him make the right decisions.

## THINK

1. How was Saul chosen to be king? 2. What did Saul do to show that he could make good decisions for God? 3. Every time you must choose something you must decide. Why should you ask God or parents to help you decide?

## LEARN

From this story, you learn that you can decide the right way when God helps you. Ask Him!

## DO

Draw a stoplight on a card. Put in a red light only. Draw a second one and put in the green light only. Put these up in your room to remind you to say yes (green light) to things that will please God and parents, and to say no (red light) to things that will not please them.

# David is Chosen to be King

*A Story about* WISDOM

"I have chosen a new king for Israel," God told Samuel one day. "Saul was once a good king when he trusted Me to help him. But now Saul does not obey Me, so he cannot continue to be king."

Samuel listened to God. He knew that God's ways were wise. "Go to Bethlehem and see Jesse," God told Samuel. "I will show you which of his sons will become Israel's next king."

The people of Bethlehem were surprised to see the great prophet Samuel entering their small town. "Is there anything wrong?" the town leaders asked. "Everything is fine," Samuel replied. "We will have a feast together and worship God. Invite all the people."

Jesse and seven of his sons went to the feast. But David, the youngest, stayed home to watch the sheep. Samuel told Jesse that some day one of his sons would be the next king of Israel. Today God would show Samuel which son it would be.

Jesse asked his sons to walk before Samuel. The first and oldest was Eliab. Because he was tall and handsome, Samuel thought, "This must be the man God has chosen." But God said that He looks at a person's heart, not at his appearance. Each son stood before Samuel, but not one was the man God had chosen.

"Are these all the sons you have?" Samuel asked. "I have one more," Jesse said. "But he is just a boy, watching the sheep." Jesse sent for this boy David to come to Samuel.

When Samuel saw David coming, God told him that this was the one He had chosen to be Israel's next king. If Samuel could have looked into the future, he would have seen that God was making a wise choice. Samuel was glad that God sees things as they really are. Aren't you?

## THINK

1. When Samuel looked at Jesse's oldest son, why did he think he would make a good king? Why was he wrong? What did God see? 2. Which is wiser, to look at someone's appearance, or to see his "heart," the way he really is? Why?

## LEARN

From this story, you learn that it is wiser to see things as they really are, not as they appear to be. Good looks do not make a good heart.

## DO

Pretend this week that each person you see is wearing a mask. Now try to get to know the person behind the mask. You may be surprised to find what a friend that person can be!

# David and Goliath

## A Story about TRUST

"Take some food to your brothers," Jesse told his son David one day. "And please find out if they are all right."

David wanted to fight in the army with his three older brothers. But he was the youngest, so he had to take care of the family sheep.

When David reached the camp he could tell that something was wrong and asked why. "See for yourself," said a soldier, pointing across the stream toward the Philistine camp.

There was the biggest man David had ever seen. "That is Goliath," the soldier said. "Listen to him!" Goliath walked to the edge of the stream and shouted at the Israelite army. "Send one man to fight me," he dared. "If I kill him, you must all become our slaves. If he kills me, we will become your slaves."

David was angry when he heard Goliath. "I will fight that giant myself," David cried. The soldiers heard David and took him to King Saul. "You can't do that!" the king said. "You are too young."

But David would not give up. "God helped me kill lions and bears when they attacked my sheep. And God will help me defeat this giant." Saul was amazed at the boy's trust in God. So he sent him to fight Goliath.

David knelt by the stream and picked up five smooth stones. Then he went to meet Goliath. The giant laughed when he saw this young man. But David shouted, "You have a sword, a spear, and a shield on your side. But I have the God of heaven and earth on my side."

David slipped a stone into his sling-shot, whirled it around his head, and let the stone fly. It hit Goliath on the forehead and he dropped to the ground. That day the Israelite soldiers learned an important lesson. God helps those who trust Him.

## THINK

1. Why were the soldiers of Israel afraid of Goliath? 2. Why wasn't David afraid of him? 3. How did David fight him? 4. Why do you think David won?

## LEARN

From this story, you learn that God helps those who trust Him.

## DO

Ask if this is right: A little person with big trust is bigger than a big person with little trust. What will you do about it?

# Saul Tries to Kill David

## A Story about LOYALTY

"Kill David!" Saul shouted at his son Jonathan and the palace attendants. Saul was afraid of David because God helped David in whatever he did. This made David famous and Saul jealous. Saul did not follow God anymore, so he wanted to kill David.

One day Saul was troubled. He needed some quiet music to calm him. David was a good musician, so he brought his harp into the palace to play for Saul. But still the king was not happy. Suddenly he hurled his spear at David. David ducked, then escaped from the palace. Saul and his men followed David all the way to Samuel's house in Ramah. There God stopped Saul from following David for awhile.

David hurried to find his best friend Jonathan. "I have always tried to be loyal to your father and please him," David explained. "So why is he trying to kill me? Now I must run away and hide."

Jonathan and David thought of a plan. "I will ask my father if he is really trying to kill you," Jonathan replied. "If he is, I will help you run away."

David hid by a field while Jonathan went to talk with King Saul. "You must leave at once," Jonathan said when he returned. "My father Saul wants to kill you." So David ran away into the wilderness. David could have fought Saul and become king. But David was loyal to Saul because God had made him king.

David found a cave in the hills and lived there. Other men came to live with David and made David their leader. When Saul learned that David was gone, he called together his best soldiers and hunted for David.

Saul kept looking for David whenever he could. Once Saul sat at the opening of a cave. He did not know that David was inside the cave. David could have killed Saul and become king. But he didn't. David knew that he would be king someday, but he wanted to let God decide the right time.

Once David crept into Saul's camp at night. While the king was sleeping, David took his spear and water jug. One of David's soldiers was going to kill Saul, but David stopped him.

As long as Saul lived, David served him faithfully because God had chosen Saul to be king. David was loyal to the one God had put in charge, and that made David loyal to God.

## THINK

1. Why did Saul try to kill David? 2. What did David do? 3. Who has God put in charge of our lives? Why should we be loyal to them?

## LEARN

From this story, you learn that you should be loyal to those God has placed over you.

## DO

Ask three people who they are most loyal to. Then ask yourself the same question. Did any of them say parents? Did any say God? What does this tell you?

# David Brings the Ark to Jerusalem

## A Story about JOY

What a day this would be! King David had made plans to bring the Ark of the Covenant into Jerusalem, the capital city. It was about time! This beautiful golden chest had been in a man's home for many years. Now the king thought it should be in Jerusalem.

Everyone was excited when the king had the Ark put into an ox cart. The procession set out for Jerusalem in a happy mood. Then something happened. When one of the oxen stumbled, a man reached out to steady the Ark and keep it from falling. When he touched the Ark, he fell to the ground dead. King David was so sad. He had the Ark put in another home. Then he went back to Jerusalem.

During the next three months, David tried to find out what had happened. Then he knew. He had forgotten to look in God's Word to see how the Ark should be moved. He studied carefully what God said. He would move the Ark the way God wanted.

So David and his people set out again to move the Ark to Jerusalem. This time they did exactly what God said.

You should have heard the shouts of joy and the sounds of the trumpets. The air was filled with joy. But one person was not happy that day. King Saul's daughter Michal, who was also David's wife, was angry and jealous. When she looked from her window and saw David dancing with joy as he brought the Ark into the city, she hated him. And when he came home she began to argue with him about the way he danced in the streets with joy.

What a sad ending that was to a wonderful day. Michal was jealous and angry while everyone else was filled with joy.

But the Ark was where it should have been. King David placed it in a special tent and made many sacrifices to God. Then he gave food to every person who had come to share this wonderful day with him.

Most important, David's heart was full of joy that day because he had moved the Ark the way God wanted. That's the way to find joy in all that we do.

# THINK

1. Why did things go wrong the first time the Ark was moved? 2. Why did things go right the next time? 3. Why was this such a day of joy?

# LEARN

From this story, you learn that joy comes from doing things the way God wants them done.

# DO

Cut out a round piece of cardboard like a big coin. One one side draw a smiling face. On the other side draw a sad face. When you do something that you think pleases God, put the smiling face up. When you do something you think does not please Him, put the sad face up. What will this remind you to do?

# The Queen of Sheba Visits Solomon

## A Story about WISDOM

"Who is this wise king?" the Queen of Sheba wondered. She had heard many stories of a great king named Solomon who had riches and wisdom beyond measure. "It is a long journey, but I must travel to Israel and see this man," the queen thought. "I must see how wise he really is."

After many days of travel, the tired queen entered the gates of Jerusalem where King Solomon lived. Following her was a camel caravan with the finest gifts her country had to offer.

King Solomon was waiting for the queen. He invited her into his splendid palace and showed her everything he had. When the Queen of Sheba saw the beautiful city, the storehouses full of gold, and the billiant jewels, she could hardly speak.

The queen soon learned that Solomon was as wise as he was rich. She asked him every kind of difficult question, but the king always replied with a clear and simple answer.

The queen watched each day as King Solomon offered sweet-smelling sacrifices to God at the temple. The temple was the most magnificent building in the land of Israel, and Solomon had built it in worship and honor to the Lord.

At last it was time for the queen to go home. "Praise be to your God for making you king," she said to Solomon. That's what Solomon's people must have thought, too, for they were glad that God had given them such a wise king.

## THINK

1. Who came to see King Solomon? Why did she come? 2. How did the queen know that Solomon was wise? 3. What did she say before she went home?

## LEARN

From this story, you learn that Solomon was a wise king. That is because he had asked God to make him wise. Perhaps you should ask God to make you wise too.

## DO

Read Proverbs 9:10. It tells you that you must love and respect the Lord before you can be wise. You will become wise as you read God's Word and pray to Him each day. Will you do that?

# God Takes Care of Elijah

## *A Story about* PROVIDING

"You are a wicked man," the prophet Elijah told King Ahab. "That is because you do not follow God. But God will show you how great He is. He will keep it from raining in Israel for a long time."

Ahab really was a wicked man. Since King Solomon died, many of Israel's kings would not follow God. Ahab was one of the worst. He prayed to idols of wood and stone. He even married Jezebel, a wicked woman who tried to kill those who worshiped God. But Elijah loved God and trusted Him to provide for him.

Ahab was angry at Elijah for stopping the rain. He wanted to hurt Elijah. So God told Elijah to hide.

Elijah found a little stream by the desert, where he had water to drink and a place to sleep. Ahab would not find him there. But what would Elijah eat? Elijah knew when he saw a big black raven flying toward him, bringing bread and meat in its bill. Each day the raven brought bread and meat for Elijah to eat. God had sent the raven to provide for Elijah.

At last the stream dried up and there was no water to drink. Even though it had not rained for a long time, Elijah knew that God would still take care of him. Then one day God told Elijah to go to the town of Zarephath. "There you will find a widow who will provide all the food and water you need," God said.

As Elijah entered the town gate, he saw the widow gathering sticks. "Please give me a drink of water and piece of bread," he asked her. "There is no bread left," the widow replied. "All that I have is a little jar of flour and a little jug of oil, just enough to make one last meal for myself and my son. When that is gone we will die."

"Don't be afraid," said Elijah. "God will provide for you the way He has provided for me." Then Elijah asked the widow to make a small biscuit of bread. "God says the jar of flour and the jug of oil will not become empty until it rains again in Israel," he told the widow.

Each day the widow used some flour from the jar and some oil from the jug. Each day there was enough to make bread for Elijah, the widow, and her son. Once again God provided!

## THINK

1. How did God provide for Elijah by the stream? 2. How did God provide for Elijah at the widow's home? 3. How does God provide for you each day?

## LEARN

From this story, you learn that God provides. He gives food and water and other things we need.

## DO

Look in your refrigerator. What would Elijah and the widow have thought about the food in there? Why should you never complain about the things you don't have?

# Elisha Raises a Boy to Life

## A Story about KINDNESS

Imagine not having a Bible to read! In Elisha's day, the families in Israel did not have Bibles. They had only prophets to tell them about God. So Elisha walked around Israel, telling the people how to serve God.

One day Elisha entered the small town of Shunem. A kind woman ran out of her house and asked him to stay for a meal. After that, each time Elisha passed through Shunem, the woman and her husband invited Elisha to eat with them. Soon they became good friends.

"Let's build a small room on the roof for Elisha," the woman said to her husband one day. "Then Elisha can stay with us whenever he passes through town. And we can learn more about God."

Elisha was happy when the woman showed him his new room. Later he said to his servant Gehazi, "This woman has been so kind to us. What can we do to repay her for her kindness?" Gehazi had an idea. "This woman has always wanted a son," he replied. "But she had never had one." So Elisha talked to her.

"About this time next year you will hold your son in your arms," he promised. And just as Elisha had said, the next year God gave her a baby boy.

One day, when the child grew to be a strong boy, he was helping his father in the fields. Suddenly he became very sick and died. The woman of Shunem laid the boy on Elisha's bed. Then she saddled her donkey and rode away to find the prophet.

When she saw Elisha, she fell on her knees at his feet. "I never asked for a son because I was afraid something like this would happen," she cried. Elisha gave Gehazi his staff and said, "Run to the woman's house and lay the staff on the boy's face." Gehazi ran ahead and did what Elisha told him. But nothing happened.

Soon Elisha reached the house. He went into the room alone and prayed to God. Then he lay on top of the boy. Suddenly the boy sneezed and opened his eyes!

Elisha called the woman in. When she saw her son she cried with joy. She could not stop thanking Elisha. Once again Elisha had repaid the woman for her kindness.

## THINK

1. How was the Shunammite couple kind to Elisha? 2. What did Elisha do for them? 3. Why should we be kind to others?

## LEARN

From this story, you learn that you should always be kind to others. Sometime you may need their kindness in return.

## DO

What is the most kind thing you have seen happen this week? What is the most unkind thing you have seen happen this week? Which do you think pleases God more? Why?

# Naaman Is Healed

## A Story about HUMILITY

Naaman was a very important man, the general of Syria's mighty army. But Naaman had one big problem. He was a leper, and there was no cure.

Naaman's little servant girl knew how he could get well. "Naaman can be healed if he goes to Israel and sees the great prophet," she said to his wife one day.

When Naaman heard about this prophet, he set out for Israel at once and went straight to the king. The king was frightened. "Am I God? How can I cure you?" he shouted. "Are you trying to start a fight with me?"

When the prophet Elisha heard about Naaman, he sent a message to the king. "Tell Naaman I am the man he wants to see."

Naaman jumped into his chariot and hurried to Elisha's house. "This man will do some great thing to heal me," Naaman thought as he ran to the door. But Elisha didn't even come out to see Naaman. He sent his servant instead. The servant opened the door and told Naaman, "Elisha says to wash seven times in the Jordan River and you will be healed."

Naaman stamped his foot with anger. "An important man like me should not have to wash in that dirty river," Naaman said. Then he started home. But his servants stopped him. "You want to get well, don't you?" they asked. Naaman thought about it. He was being too proud. He should do almost anything to get well, even wash in a dirty river. Do you know what happened when he stopped being proud and obeyed God's prophet? He was healed!

## THINK

1. What was wrong with Naaman? Why did he go to see God's prophet? 2. What did Elisha tell Naaman to do? Why didn't Naaman want to do it? 3. What happened when Naaman stopped being proud and obeyed God's prophet? 4. Are you ever proud? Why is God pleased more when you are not proud?

## LEARN

From this story, you learn that God can help you more when you stop being proud and let Him help you.

## DO

Read 1 Peter 5:5-6. What does God do for those who are humble? Why not pray to God now, and ask Him to help you?

# Jonah and the Big Fish

*A Story about* OBEDIENCE

"Jonah! Jonah!" Jonah sat up and listened as God spoke to him. "I have a special message for you," God said. "Go to the city of Nineveh. Tell the people that I will punish them because they do not obey Me."

Jonah was afraid to do what God said. Nineveh was one of the biggest cities in the world, in a country that did not like Israel. No wonder Jonah was frightened!

Jonah did not ask God to help him. Instead he ran away and boarded a large ship. But Jonah could not run away from God.

Out on the sea, a great storm hit and the ship was torn and battered by the winds. The sailors cried out to their gods, but of course they couldn't hear. Finally the sailors knew that Jonah was the cause of this storm. "Who are you, and what have you done to bring such trouble upon us?" they demanded.

"I am a prophet of the living God," Jonah replied. "My God is the Lord of the heaven and earth. He made the sea and dry land." Now the crew was even more afraid. "I have disobeyed God," Jonah said. "You must throw me overboard and save yourselves."

The ship was about to sink. So the sailors finally picked up Jonah and tossed him into the water. At once the sea became calm.

God sent a big fish to swallow Jonah. There in the belly of that fish Jonah learned his lesson and promised to obey God no matter what might happen to him. After three days and three nights, God spoke to the fish and it coughed Jonah up on dry land.

Jonah went straight to Nineveh to tell the people what God had said. The king listened to Jonah and was sorry for his sins. He commanded all the men and women of the city to set aside a special time to eat no food and to ask God to forgive their sins. When God saw that the people were truly sorry for the evil things they had done, He forgave them. Nineveh obeyed God and was not punished.

But Jonah wasn't happy. He thought Nineveh was so bad that God should destroy it. Jonah made a shelter outside the city and waited to see if God would change His mind. The sun grew hot, so God caused a vine to grow over Jonah's shelter to give him shade. Jonah was happy for the vine. But when the vine withered the next day, Jonah was angry that his shade was gone.

Then God spoke to Jonah. "You are concerned for this withered plant, even though you did not make it grow. Shouldn't I be

concerned about this great city with all its people? Until you came here with my message, they did not even know the difference between good and evil."

Now Jonah was sorry. When he was in the fish's belly, he had decided to obey God, and God had given him another chance. In the same way, God gave Nineveh a new chance to follow His ways.

## THINK

1. Why was Jonah running away from God? 2. How did he learn to obey? 3. Why then did Jonah want Nineveh to be destroyed? 4. How did God teach him that Nineveh should be forgiven just as Jonah had been forgiven when he obeyed? 5. Who should you obey? Why?

## LEARN

From this story, you learn that it is better to obey. You should obey God and your parents, shouldn't you?

## DO

On a sheet of paper, write OBEY on the left side, and DISOBEY on the right. Under the word OBEY, write some things God or your parents want you to do. Under DISOBEY write some things they do not want you to do. Which side is better?

# Isaiah Tells Others About God

## *A Story about* PROMISES

God wanted to do great things for His people. He gave them many wonderful promises. All they had to do was obey. That is why God sent prophets. The prophets told the people about God's promises. They taught the people how to please God and believe in His promises.

One day a man named Isaiah had a dream. In the dream God called him to be a prophet. "Isaiah," God said. "Listen to Me. Tell the people what I am about to say."

Then God began. "Long ago I promised Abraham that all the nations of the earth would one day receive My most wonderful gift. But that gift would come only through Jesus, My Son. The gift is eternal life and forgiveness for sin instead of punishment."

Isaiah told the people about God's promise that Jesus would come some day. "Please stop following idols," Isaiah begged the people. "And listen to the wonderful things God wants to do for you."

Isaiah believed God with all his heart. He believed God so much that he couldn't stop telling the people about God's goodness. It did not matter who Isaiah was talking to. It did not matter how many people made fun of him. Isaiah would never stop telling others about God and His wonderful promises.

## THINK

1. What did God promise to Abraham? 2. What special gift did God promise to His people? 3. What book has many of God's promises for you to read? Why should you read it each day and believe God's promises?

## LEARN

From this story, you learn that God has many wonderful promises, and that He keeps each of them.

## DO

Read Isaiah 53 together as a family. As you do, picture the crucifixion of Jesus. Isaiah was telling God's promise to send Jesus to die for our sins.

# Hezekiah Pleases God

## A Story about PRAYER

"King Hezekiah!" a servant shouted. "A big army is marching toward our city." Hezekiah looked. It was the army of Assyria, the strongest army in the world.

Soon a messenger came to the gates of Jerusalem. He was from the king of Assyria. "The king says that you should give up now," he told Hezekiah. "You cannot fight against us." The people of Jerusalem listened to the messenger. They were afraid. But Hezekiah said to them, "Don't be afraid. You must trust God."

Again the king of Assyria sent a messenger to Jerusalem. This time he brought a letter. Hezekiah read the letter. It said, "Hezekiah, do not trust your God to save you. I have captured many cities as big as Jerusalem. Their gods did not save them, so why do you think your God will help you? Give up now and you will be spared."

Hezekiah took the king's letter to the temple. He spread it out before God. Then Hezekiah prayed, "O Lord, the king of Asyria says that You cannot save Jerusalem. Please save us and show the Assyrians that you are the God of the whole earth."

That night God sent an angel into the army camp of Assyria. The angel killed so many soldiers that the rest ran away. God had answered Hezekiah's prayer.

Many years later Hezekiah became sick. "Soon you will die," the prophet Isaiah told him. Hezekiah was sad. "O Lord," he prayed as he lay in bed, "I have been faithful to you all of my life. I have taught the people to love You. Please do not let me die yet."

Hezekiah did not die. Once again God answered Hezekiah's prayer because he was a good king. Hezekiah was thankful that God was his friend.

## THINK

1. When the king of Assyria came, what did Hezekiah ask God to do? What did God do?
2. When Hezekiah got sick, what did he ask God to do? What did God do? 3. When you need help, who should you ask to help you? Why should you pray, instead of doing what you please?

## LEARN

From this story, you learn that God listens to your prayers.

## DO

God always listens to your prayers. He has three answers: no, yes, and wait. The next time you pray, see which answer God sends. Write PRAY on a card and put it on the door of your room. It will remind you to pray before you leave your room.

# Into the Fiery Furnace

*A Story about* COURAGE

"I am such a great king," proud Nebuchadnezzar thought to himself. "I will build a large golden statue of myself. All of the royal officials from across my kingdom must come and worship it."

Soon the king's servants were busy making the king's statue of gold. At last the big day arrived. A servant read the king's order. "When the musicians play their instruments," he read, "everyone must bow down and worship the golden statue. Anyone who does not will be thrown into a furnace of fire."

The crowd became quiet. The musicians began to play, and everyone bowed low before the statue—everyone but Shadrach, Meshach, and Abednego.

Nebuchadnezzar was both angry and sad. He liked Shadrach, Meshach, and Abednego. They were such good and honest men that Nebuchadnezzar had promoted them to high positions within his kingdom.

"Why did you not obey my order?" the king shouted. "Do you want to be thrown into the fiery furnace?"

"God is able to save us if He wants to," the men began. "But even if He doesn't save us, we will serve only the true God." What a courageous thing to say!

King Nebuchadnezzar was angry now. At his command, the soldiers threw Shadrach, Meshach, and Abednego into the blazing furnace.

But Nebuchadnezzar could not believe his eyes. Now there were four men in the furnace, and one looked like an angel! "Come out of there," yelled the king. Shadrach, Meshach, and Abednego walked safely out of the fire. Not even their clothes were burned.

"Praise the God of Shadrach, Meshach, and Abednego," the king exclaimed. "These men trust their God and do what they know is right, even when others try to stop them."

## THINK

1. Why didn't the three friends bow down before the golden statue? 2. What did the king do to them? 3. How did these three men show that they had courage to obey God? 4. Do you have the courage to do what God wants? 5. Do you have the courage to tell your friends that you love God?

## LEARN

From this story, you learn that God helps those who show courage to do what He wants.

## DO

Read Deuteronomy 31:6. What does this tell you about showing courage for God? Would you like to memorize this verse?

# Daniel in the Lion's Den

*A Story about* PRAYER

"We must catch Daniel doing something wrong," some bad men said. "Then the king will have to get rid of him." But the men could find nothing wrong with Daniel. These men hated Daniel because Darius, the new king, had just made Daniel the second most important man in the kingdom. They wanted to have Daniel's job. They would even kill him to get it.

The bad men thought of a plan. "Daniel is too good," they said. "We will never catch him doing something wrong. Let's make a law that says that everyone must pray to the king only for 30 days." The men knew that Daniel prayed to God every morning, noon, and night. And they knew that Daniel would never stop praying. Daniel loved God too much.

The men went to Darius. They bragged about him and made him feel important. Then they talked him into making the new law.

One day the men caught Daniel praying to God as usual. "Daniel is not obeying your new law," they said to the king. The king was sorry now that he had made the law. He liked Daniel and did not want to kill him. But he could not change the law. "I hope that your God, to whom you pray, will rescue you," he told Daniel. Then the men threw Daniel into a den of hungry lions.

King Darius could not sleep that night. Early in the morning he ran to the lions' den. "Daniel!" he called out. "Was your God able to save you?" The king was overjoyed when he heard Daniel's voice. God had shut the mouths of the hungry lions so Daniel was saved.

The king's men took Daniel out of the lions' den. Darius took the evil men who had tried to get Daniel killed and threw them into the lions' den. Then he made a newer law which said that everyone should honor God, for He was the true God.

## THINK

1. Why did the evil men want to hurt Daniel? 2. How did they plan to get him killed? 3. Why do you think Daniel would not stop praying? 4. Why should you keep on praying each day? Do you?

## LEARN

From this story, you learn that it is a good idea to keep on praying to God each day, no matter what happens.

## DO

Ask God to help you remember to pray. Ask your parents also to help you remember to pray.

# Queen Esther Saves Her People

*A Story about* COURAGE

"Who is the most beautiful young woman in my kingdom?" King Ahasuerus wondered. The king wanted to find a new queen, so he sent his servants to bring many beautiful women to see him. He would choose one to be his queen.

One of the young women was a Jewish girl named Esther. Her uncle Mordecai took care of her. When the king decided to make Esther his queen, Mordecai came to the palace gate to hear news about her.

Each morning a wicked man named Haman rode through the palace gate. He was a very important man, so people bowed down before him. But Mordecai would not bow down. He believed that he should bow down only to God.

Haman was furious. He made plans to have all of the Jewish people in the land killed. He knew that included Mordecai, but he did not know that it included Queen Esther.

Mordecai learned about Haman's evil plan. He told Queen Esther she must do something about it. But what? Esther could not even go to see the king without being asked. If she did, the king could kill her for doing it.

Esther wondered what she should do. Then she decided. She would go to see the king. That was a very brave thing to do. Esther knew she was risking her life to save her people.

When the king saw Esther, he held out his golden scepter. That told her that he would not kill her. Instead, he listened to her. Then the king stopped the wicked Haman from killing Queen Esther, Mordecai and their people. Now Esther was glad that she had the courage to go to the king.

## THINK

1. Why did Haman want to kill Mordecai and his people? 2. How did Esther stop him? 3. How did Esther show that she had courage? 4. What are some ways you can show courage to do what God wants?

## LEARN

From this story, you learn that Esther had courage and saved her people. Showing courage may help you please God more, or help someone know Him better. That's worth doing, isn't it?

## DO

Choose the words that you think relate to Esther: COURAGE, AFRAID, BRAVE, COWARD, TIMID, WEAK, UNAFRAID.

102

# John the Baptist Is Born

## *A Story about* PROMISES

Zacharias was excited as he walked to the temple. Each day he worked there as a priest. But this was a special day, for Zacharias had been chosen to enter the holy room of the temple. A priest was happy if he was chosen to do this once during his lifetime.

As Zacharias walked into the holy room, the people waited outside. Zacharias had never been in there before. He looked around and saw the golden altar where he would burn incense and pray to God.

Suddenly an angel stood next to the altar. Zacharias put his hands over his face and cried with fear. "Don't be afraid," said the angel. "God knows that you have wanted a baby for a long time. He has heard your prayers. Soon you and Elizabeth will have a baby boy!"

Then the angel reminded Zacharias of a special promise God had made. Ever since the time of Abraham, God had promised His people He would send His Son, the Messiah, to save people from their sins. Many had forgotten God's promise. But God always keeps His promises. He makes things happen at the right time. Now was the right time. But before God's Son would come, someone had to make things ready for Him.

Zacharias' son would be the one to prepare the people for the coming of God's Son.

Some months later Elizabeth had this special baby boy. "Will you call him Zacharias?" the neighbors asked. "No, his name will be John," she answered. "Is that what you want to name him, too?" they asked Zacharias. But Zacharias had not been able to speak since the angel had come to see him. So they brought Zacharias a clay writing tablet and he wrote, "His name is John." As soon as he had written this, God let Zacharias speak again.

Everyone knew that John was a special baby. Now God was ready to fulfill His great promise to send His Son.

---

### THINK

1. Why was this a special day for Zacharias? 2. What did the angel tell him? 3. What was his baby going to do when he grew up? 4. What was the baby's name?

---

### LEARN

From this story, you learn that God keeps His promises.

---

### DO

John later had a longer name. Do you know what it was? Look up Luke 7:20 and you will find out.

# Jesus Is Born

*A Story about* JOY

One day Joseph heard some bad news. The Roman emperor wanted to count all the people of the land. That meant Joseph and Mary would have to leave their home in Nazareth for a few days and travel to Bethlehem, the town where their family had lived.

The journey was hard, especially for Mary, for she was going to have a baby. At last they arrived at the small Bethlehem inn. But there was no more room, only a stable where the animals slept. There in the stable Mary had a baby, and named Him Jesus.

At the same time, shepherds were taking care of their sheep on a hill near Bethlehem. As they looked into the night sky, an angel appeared above them. "Do not be afraid," the angel said. "Tonight I have good news that will bring great joy to all people. Tonight Jesus the Savior was born in Bethlehem. Hurry and you will find Him lying in a manger."

Suddenly the sky was filled with angels praising God. "Glory to God in the heavens," they said. "And peace to men on earth." When the angels were gone, the shepherds hurried into Bethlehem and found Jesus where the angel said He would be. When they saw Him, they knew that He was God's Son, and they were filled with joy.

Then the shepherds went back to their sheep, telling everyone along the way what they had seen. Everyone who listened to the shepherds was filled with joy. God was pleased too, for He knew that it was the right time for His Son to bring joy to the world.

## THINK

1. Why did Joseph and Mary go to Bethlehem? 2. What wonderful thing happened while they were there? 3. Why were the shepherds filled with joy? 4. Why should Jesus' birth bring joy to you too?

## LEARN

From this story, you learn that Jesus' birth brings joy to you, as it did to the shepherds. Like the shepherds, tell others about Jesus so they may have this joy too.

## DO

Across a piece of paper, write the three letters J O Y. Using the same O, write Y above it, and U below it to spell Y O U. Jesus brings JOY to YOU. Put this in your room to remind you of this truth.

# Wise Men Visit Jesus

*A Story about* REVERENCE

When Jesus was born, God put a big bright star in the sky over Bethlehem. Far away, wise men saw this beautiful star. "What could it mean?" they wondered. At last they learned that the star was a sign that a great king had been born. "We must find this wonderful king," the wise men said.

Day after day, the wise men followed the star. After many days they came to Jerusalem and went to see King Herod. They did not know that Herod was a wicked man. "Where is the great king who has been born?" they asked Herod. "We want to worship him."

Herod frowned, for he did not want another king to take his place. Quickly Herod talked to some teachers who knew the Bible well. "Where does your Bible say this king will be born?" he demanded. "In the town of Bethlehem," they answered.

So Herod sent the wise men to Bethlehem. "Let me know when you find the child," he said. "I want to worship Him, too." But Herod really wanted to kill Jesus.

In Bethlehem the wise men saw the star shining over a certain house. When they went into the house and saw the baby Jesus, they bowed down to worship Him. Then they gave Him wonderful gifts, gold, frankincense, and myrrh. These were gifts that even a king would like.

That night the wise men had a dream. God told them that Herod wanted to kill Jesus. So the next morning the wise men began their long journey home on a different road. As they went, they thanked God for leading them to this great King so they could worship Him.

## THINK

1. What did the wise men see? 2. Why do you think God put the bright star in the sky? 3. What did the wise men do when they saw Jesus? 4. What should we do when we talk to Jesus?

## LEARN

From this story, you learn reverence, or honor, for Jesus because He is God's Son, and you should worship Him.

## DO

The next time you pray, think about some different things that you do. Do you close your eyes? Do you bow your head? Do you get down on your knees sometimes? These are ways people use to honor, or reverence, Jesus.

# Jesus Talks With Temple Teachers

*A Story about* WISDOM

"It's time to go to the big feast in Jerusalem," Joseph said to his wife Mary. Jesus was twelve this year, and was anxious to go to the Passover Feast, too. Each year many people traveled to Jerusalem to enjoy the feast together and to worship God in the temple.

Joseph, Mary and Jesus traveled the long road from Nazareth to Jerusalem with their friends and neighbors. When all the people went together it was called a caravan. This made the trip safer and easier.

Jesus must have been excited when his family came at last to the city. Jerusalem was big, and there were many beautiful houses and buildings. But the most beautiful building was the temple, where the most important part of the Passover Feast took place.

The great feast lasted for seven days. When it was time to leave, all the people from Nazareth got together and began the long trip home. After they stopped for the night, Joseph and Mary looked for Jesus. They thought he was with friends in another part of the caravan. But Jesus was not there. "He must be lost back in Jerusalem," they said. Of course they were worried.

Joseph and Mary left the caravan and hurried back to Jerusalem. Where was Jesus?

They kept looking, getting more worried as time passed. When they went to the temple, they found Jesus talking with some wise teachers. They were asking Jesus many difficult questions, and Jesus was answering them all. The teachers were amazed that Jesus was so wise. That was because He was God's Son.

"Where have you been?" Joseph and Mary asked Jesus. "We have been looking everywhere for you."

"I have been here in the temple," Jesus answered. Then Jesus went home with them. Even God's Son obeyed His parents.

## THINK

1. Where did Mary and Joseph find Jesus? 2. What was Jesus doing there? 3. Why was He so wise? 4. Why should you listen to Jesus?

## LEARN

From this story, you learn that it is important to listen to Jesus because He is God's Son, and is so wise.

## DO

Ask your parents or your pastor to let you see a red-letter edition of the Bible. It has all of Jesus' words printed in red. It will help you see how much Jesus said, which you may read.

# Jesus Is Baptized

*A Story about* HUMILITY

John, that special baby which Zacharias and Elizabeth had, was now a man. Everyone called him John the Baptist. He lived in the wild country. John often talked with God and God helped him do many things.

One day God told John to go to the Jordan River. There John preached that Jesus the Messiah would soon be with them. "You must be sorry for your sins," John told them. "And then you must try not to sin anymore." John baptized those who truly were sorry for their sins.

It seemed as if everyone wanted to listen to John. Every day more and more people gathered by the river to hear what he said.

Priests from the temple in Jerusalem came to ask him questions. "Are you the Messiah, God's Son, the one we have been waiting for?" they asked him. "No I am not," he replied. "Then are you a great prophet?" they asked. John answered, "I am only a messenger for God. I am trying to help you get ready for the Messiah to come, which will be soon."

One day Jesus came to talk to John at the Jordan River. Jesus was now a man, too. He wanted John to baptize Him, even though He had never sinned, so John did what Jesus asked. When Jesus stepped from the water, John heard God's voice from heaven, "This is My Son, whom I love."

Now John knew for sure that Jesus was God's Son. Jesus would soon begin to teach and help the people. John knew also that Jesus must become more important, while he became less important. It is not easy to cheerfully let someone become more important than you. But John was willing to put Jesus first because that is the way a humble man does it.

## THINK

1. What did John tell the people to do? 2. What did John say about Jesus? 3. Why did John want to make Jesus look more important than himself? 4. Is Jesus first in your life?

## LEARN

From this story, you learn that humility is putting Jesus first in your life.

## DO

Write JESUS on a piece of paper. Under His name, write OTHERS. Under that write YOU. Now write the first letter of each word—J O Y. That's what you have when you put JESUS first, OTHERS next, and YOU last.

# Jesus Calls His First Disciples

## A Story about FOLLOWING

Two men stood by the Jordan River, talking with John the Baptist. Suddenly John looked toward the path that passed nearby and pointed toward Jesus. "Look," he said. "There is the Lamb of God." That was a way of saying that Jesus was God's Son. When the two men heard what John said, they followed Jesus.

All that day the men listened as Jesus told them many wonderful things about God. Andrew, one of the men, hurried to find his brother Simon. "I have seen the Messiah," he said. When Jesus saw Simon coming, he said to him, "Your name is Simon. But from now on it will be Peter." Peter must have been amazed that Jesus even knew his name.

The next day Jesus decided to go home to Galilee. As He was leaving He met Philip. "Follow Me!" He said to Philip, and Philip decided to follow Jesus. Philip asked his friend Nathanael to come, too. When Nathanael met Jesus he was surprised to hear Jesus say his name. "How do you know me?" Nathanael asked. "I saw you before Philip found you, sitting under a fig tree," Jesus replied. "You really are the Son of God," Nathanael said. So Nathanael followed Jesus, too.

Back home in Galilee, as they were walking along the Sea of Galilee, Jesus saw Peter and Andrew again, fishing from their boat. "Follow Me, and I will make you fishers of men," Jesus said. At once Peter and Andrew pulled their nets into the boat, rowed to shore, and followed Jesus.

Then Jesus saw James and John, two other brothers, fishing. "Follow Me," Jesus said to them. James and John said goodbye to their father and followed Jesus.

Can't you see these men, who were called disciples, walking with Jesus? Following Jesus was the most important thing they could do.

## THINK

1. What did Jesus ask these men to do? 2. What did they do? 3. How would you like to have been with these men when they went with Jesus? What would you like to have asked Jesus?

## LEARN

From this story, you learn that the most important thing you can do is follow Jesus. Will you?

## DO

How can you follow Jesus? List 5 of the most important things you should do when you follow Him. List 5 of the most important things you should not do when you follow Him.

115

# Jesus Turns Water Into Wine

## *A Story about* OBEDIENCE

The little town of Cana was filled with excitement as friends and neighbors prepared for a wedding. The bride and groom made last minute arrangements as servants busily prepared the food and carried it into the banquet room.

Jesus and His disciples were invited to the wedding. So was Mary, Jesus' mother. The wedding feast went on for several days. One day the wine was gone.

Mary told Jesus what had happened. Then she spoke to the servants. "Do whatever He tells you," she said. She knew that if they obeyed Jesus, something good would happen.

Jesus pointed to six large stone water jars standing along the wall. "Fill those jars with water," He told the servants. The servants did not understand, but they obeyed Jesus and filled the jars to the very brim with water.

Then Jesus told the servants to dip their cups into the water jars and take them to the man in charge of the banquet. Once again the servants obeyed, and to their amazement found that each water jar was filled with wine! The surprised servants handed this wine to the man in charge.

The bridegroom did not know where this wine came from. But the servants knew. They were glad they had obeyed Jesus.

## THINK

1. What would have happened if the servants had refused to obey Jesus? 2. Jesus' miracle showed His great power over all things. But it also depended upon the belief and obedience of others. That is something to think about when we want a miracle in our lives.

## LEARN

From this story, you learn the importance of OBEDIENCE.

## DO

Read 1 Samuel 15:22. Then write down three ways that you can obey God today. Don't forget to ask God to help you with them. When the day is over look at your list again. How well have you followed it? Do this same thing for one week to get in the habit of remembering to obey God.

# Jesus Cleanses the Temple

*A Story about* REVERENCE

Jerusalem was filled with excitement. Each year thousands of people came here to celebrate the great Passover Feast. Some came from nearby cities. Others came from distant lands. But when they arrived in Jerusalem, they all went to the temple to worship God.

When Jesus and His disciples came to the Passover Feast, they went to the temple too. But Jesus did not like what He saw in the temple courtyard. There were cows and sheep and doves in big cages. And there were greedy looking men sitting behind tables with piles of money. These men sold birds and animals so the people could make an offering to God. But they cheated the people. They wanted to get lots of money.

Jesus was angry. "This is God's house," He shouted at the men who were selling the cows, sheep, and doves. "This is where we worship Him. I will not let you turn God's house into a marketplace."

Then Jesus made a whip from some pieces of rope. He chased the cows and sheep from the temple courtyard. He chased the men who were selling the cages of doves. Then He knocked over the tables with the piles of money. He told the greedy men to get out of God's house.

The men were angry at Jesus, but they did not try to stay. Quickly they picked up their money that had fallen on the ground. Then they ran from the temple courtyard, looking for their cows and sheep. Jesus watched them go. This was God's house. This was His Father's house, where people came to worship Him! It was not the right place for a market.

## THINK

1. What were people supposed to do at the temple? 2. What were the greedy men doing? 3. Why was Jesus angry? Why should we honor and reverence the place where we go to worship God?

## LEARN

From this story, you learn that it is important to have reverence for God's house, because that is where we go to worship God.

## DO

Hang one of your church bulletins in your room. It will remind you to thank God for your church each day this week.

# Jesus Heals a Man's Son

*A Story about* FAITH

"Jesus is here again!" people shouted in the streets of Cana. Jesus had been in the little town of Cana before, when He turned the water into wine. The people were glad to see Jesus again. What wonderful thing would He do this time?

The news that Jesus was in Cana soon reached a visitor from Capernaum. This important man, an official of the government, had a son who was so sick that he was ready to die.

The official hurried to Jeesus as fast as he could. when he found Him he fell at His feet and begged, "Please come with me and heal my son. He is sick and I am afraid that he will die."

"Do you need to see more miracles before you will believe in Me?" Jesus asked. "I do not need to see any more miracles," the man replied. "I believe you can do anything that you say you can do. And I know that you can heal my son."

Jesus was pleased that the official had so much faith. "Go back to your home," Jesus told him. "Your son will live." So the man started home, believing that Jesus would keep His word.

While he was still on his way home his servants met him. "Your son is well," they exclaimed with joy. "That is wonderful news," the official said. "Can you tell me at what time he got better?" "Yesterday, about one o'clock," they answered. The man smiled. That was the exact time that Jesus told him his son would live.

The official was glad he believed in Jesus. And when his family saw the man hug his son who was healed, they believed in Jesus too.

## THINK

1. What did the official ask Jesus to do? 2. Why did he go home before he knew that his son was well? 3. What do you believe Jesus can do for you?

## LEARN

From this story, you learn that faith in God is believing that whatever He tells you will happen, will really happen.

## DO

Ask your mother or father to read Hebrews 11 aloud. How many of these Bible people had faith in God?

# The Miracle of Fish

## A Story about OBEDIENCE

"Let's go fishing tonight," Peter said to his brother Andrew. They climbed into their fishing boat and sailed out onto the deep water of the Sea of Galilee. James and John sailed out with them.

All night the four men fished, throwing their big nets into the water and pulling them up to the side of the boat. They tried again and again but didn't catch a single fish.

When it was morning, the tired men sailed back to shore and began to wash their nets. Soon they looked up and saw Jesus coming with a crowd of people following Him.

Jesus walked toward Peter. "May I talk to the people from your boat?" He asked. Peter gladly helped Jesus into the boat and pushed it a little way from the shore. Now all the people could see and hear Jesus. After He talked with them a long time about God, it was time for the people to go home.

Then Jesus said to Peter and Andrew, "Sail out onto the sea and catch some fish." Peter shook his head and said, "Master, we fished all night, and did not catch a thing. But if you want us to go fishing, we will go."

Peter and Andrew obeyed Jesus and sailed back out to sea. They threw their net over the side of the boat. Suddenly the net was so full of fish that they could not pull it in. "Hurry and help us," they called to James and John who were in another boat.

It took all four men to pull the net from the water. Both boats were filled with so many fish that they almost sank. Peter was afraid. "You are so great," he said to Jesus. "And I am such a sinful man." But Jesus said to Peter, "Don't be afraid. From now on you will go fishing for men." Because Peter believed and obeyed Jesus, he was now ready to work for Jesus they way he should.

## THINK

1. How did Peter and Andrew obey Jesus? 2. What happened when they did? 3. What will happen when you obey Jesus?

## LEARN

From this story, you learn that God will do great and wonderful things for you when you obey Him.

## DO

Draw a simple fish to put near each plate at dinner tonight. Ask each family member to tell one important way to obey Jesus, and write it on the fish. Keep these fish for a week and ask if each person obeyed.

# Jesus Heals at the Pool of Bethesda

*A Story about* COMPASSION

There was a story going around Jerusalem that people could be healed at the Pool of Bethesda. Some said that an angel stirred the water at certain times, and that the person who stepped into the water first would be healed.

People in Jesus' time had no hospitals, good doctors, or good medicines, so they had almost no hope of getting well. So, many sick people came here to the pool and sat beside it, waiting for the water to stir.

One day Jesus noticed a certain man sitting beside the pool. The poor man had not been able to walk for 38 years. Jesus felt sorry for him, or had compassion for him.

"Do you want to get well?" Jesus asked the man. "Oh, yes, but I have no one to help me into the pool at the right time," the man answered. "Someone always gets there first."

"Lift your mat and walk home," Jesus told the man. WALK home? How could he? He had not walked for 38 years. But somehow the man believed Jesus. At once he stood up and walked away.

Later Jesus saw this same man at the temple. "You are well now, and I am happy about that," Jesus told him. "But you must do the things that please God. Sin will get you into trouble again, and it will be worse next time."

The man listened to Jesus. He had seen the love and compassion in Jesus' eyes and knew that he should do what Jesus said. He certainly did not want to be a sick man, sitting by the pool for many more years.

A man with that much compassion might never come by again.

## THINK

1. Why was the man sitting by the pool? What did he hope would happen? 2. What did Jesus say to the man? How do you think the man felt when he could suddenly walk after 38 years? 3. What do you think the man saw when he looked into Jesus' eyes? 4. Where have you seen compassion in someone's eyes before?

## LEARN

From this story, you learn that Jesus had love and compassion for people who needed Him. When you need Him, He has love and compassion for you too.

## DO

Look at your eyes in a mirror. Say something angry. How do your eyes look? Now say something loving, with compassion. Now how do your eyes look? Which do you like better? Why?

# Jesus Raises a Widow's Son

*A Story about* COMPASSION

Life had been very hard for the poor widow of Nain. But she had a son whom she loved very much. As he grew to be a strong young man, he took care of her, and that made her happy.

But one day the widow's son died. Some neighbors carried him out of the town. The widow and her friends followed, crying.

When Jesus saw the woman crying, He felt compassion toward her. "Don't cry," He said. He stopped the men who were carrying her son and looked at him. "Get up!" He said. Instantly the widow's son sat up and began to talk with his mother.

All the people praised God because Jesus showed compassion to the poor widow.

## THINK

1. What did Jesus do to help the poor widow and her son? 2. How do you show compassion toward people who hurt?

## LEARN

From this story, you learn that Jesus cares when people hurt, and we should have compassion too.

## DO

Which of these show compassion? 1. Let me help you. 2. Stop bugging me. 3. Get out of here.

# Jesus Heals the Centurion's Servant

*A Story about* FAITH

The centurion, a Roman soldier in Capernaum, had many servants. One day one of them became very sick. The centurion sent his friends to ask Jesus to come and heal his servant. "I know He can," he said.

The friends begged Jesus to come. "The centurion is a kind man," they told Him.

Before they reached the centurion's house, he sent a message out to Jesus. "Lord, I am not good enough to have You enter my house," it said. "Please just say the word, and I know my servant will be healed."

Jesus was amazed. He turned and asked the people who were following, "Do you see the faith of this man? He is a Roman soldier, and yet he believes in Me more than you do." He sent the centurion's friends back to the house where they found the servant alive and well.

## THINK

1. What did the centurion want Jesus to do? 2. Why would Jesus want you to have faith in Him?

## LEARN

From this story, you learn that Jesus can do good things for you when you believe in Him.

## DO

Would you like to memorize 2 Corinthians 5:7?

127

# Parable of the Sower

## *A Story about* LISTENING

Jesus was a splendid teacher. Every day crowds followed Him, listening for more wonderful things about God. One day Jesus stood teaching by the Sea of Galilee. But there were too many people, so He climbed into a boat and went out a little way. From the boat Jesus told the people this story.

"A farmer went out to plant some seeds. He reached into his bag and began to throw the seed this way and that way.

"Some seeds fell on the path that led to the field. The path was hard and the birds ate the seeds before they could take root.

"Some seeds fell on the stony ground. They began to grow and little plants sprang up. But the roots could not make their way through the stones to the ground below. When the hot sun came up, the little plants withered and died.

"Some seeds fell among weeds and thistles. Once again the seeds began to grow and little plants sprang up. But the weeds and thorns grew faster. They smothered the little plants until they died.

"But some seeds fell into good ground. The seeds began to grow and little plants sprang up. This time the plants grew and grew. The roots went deep into the soil, and soon the plants became big and strong. They produced a wonderful crop, with each plant having many seeds of its own for the farmer to use next spring."

Jesus had finished His story. "But what does it mean?" the disciples asked Him.

"The seed is God's Word, and the ground is the hearts of those people who hear God's Word," Jesus replied.

"God's Word cannot grow in hard hearts, just as seed cannot grow in hard ground. It cannot grow in hearts too filled with things that choke it. But it will grow in hearts that receive it."

The people listened to Jesus. And they listened to God's Word as He gave it to them. Will you?

## THINK

1. What story did Jesus tell? 2. What did Jesus say the seed was? 3. What did He say the ground was? 4. When people read God's Word to you, or when you read it, what should you do? Do you listen carefully?

## LEARN

From this story, you learn that it is good to listen to God's Word, the Bible.

## DO

Put your Bible in a box and wrap string or tape around it. Pretend for a few moments that you can never read the Bible again. How do you feel? Now unwrap it. How do you feel to see your Bible in the right place again?

129

# Jesus Raises Jarius' Daughter

## A Story about TRUST

Jairus was worried. His daughter was sick...so sick that she was dying.

"What am I going to do?" Jairus said to his wife. Suddenly he remembered that Jesus was in town.

Jairus ran from the house and headed toward the lake, where Jesus often taught. There was Jesus, with a crowd around Him.

Jairus was an important man in town, the leader of the synagogue, where the people went to worship God. But even important people need help, and only Jesus could help Jairus.

Jairus pushed his way through the crowd and fell at Jesus' feet. "Please Sir," he begged, "My daughter is sick and I know that only You can heal her. Please come with me."

Jesus was glad that Jairus trusted Him. He smiled and walked with Jairus toward his house. But soon they met one of Jairus' servants who told them that the little girl was already dead. "Trust Me," Jesus whispered.

Jairus walked sadly with Jesus into his home. Everyone there was crying. "Stop crying," said Jesus. "She is only sleeping."

Jesus took the girl's hand and spoke to her. Suddenly she stood up and smiled at her mother and father. Jairus could hardly believe his eyes! But he had trusted Jesus and now things were right again. Can't you see Jairus and his wife hugging their daughter now?

## THINK

1. Why was Jairus worried? 2. How do you know that he trusted Jesus? 3. What did Jesus do for Jairus? 4. Why should you trust Jesus?

## LEARN

From this story, you learn that good things happen when you trust Jesus.

## DO

Draw a happy face on a card. Beside it draw a sad face. Write the word TRUST under the happy face. What word should you put under the sad face? This will remind you to trust Jesus.

answered, "Even a rich man could not buy enough bread to feed them all."

"Here is a boy with five loaves of bread and two fishes," Peter said. "But what good will that do with all these people?"

"Tell the people to sit down on the grass," Jesus told His disciples. Then Jesus took the loaves of bread from the boy, thanked God for them and broke them. The disciples gave the bread to the people. Jesus did the same thing with the fish. Back and forth the disciples went, passing out the pieces of bread and fish to all the people.

At last the people were finished. The 5000 people had eaten all the food they wanted. When the disciples gathered the leftover food, there was enough to fill twelve baskets.

Jesus had used a little boy's meal to provide a multitude with food! How wonderful that Jesus takes care of those who trust in Him.

## THINK

1. How did Jesus provide for the people during the long day? 2. How did Jesus provide for the people when it was time to eat? 3. How does Jesus provide for you?

## LEARN

From this story, you learn that Jesus will always provide for those who trust Him.

## DO

Cut out magazine pictures of things that God provides, such as food, clothing, house, and furniture. What else can you find? Paste these pictures on a sheet of paper to remind you that God provides.

133

# Jesus Walks on Water

*A Story about* FAITH

It was late when the crowds began to leave, and Jesus was very tired. All day He had taught the people about God. Then He had fed the 5000 people with a young boy's lunch.

Now Jesus wanted to be alone to talk with God. "Sail your boat across the Sea of Galilee," He told His disciples. "I will go into the hills to pray."

When night came, the disciples were in the middle of the lake. The wind began to blow and strong waves rocked that tiny boat. Suddenly one disciple cried out. "A ghost!" he shouted. When the other disciples looked, they saw a man walking on the water towards them. "Don't be afraid, it is I," a voice shouted above the roaring wind. The voice sounded like Jesus. But was it?

Peter wanted to know. "Lord, if it is You, let me walk to You on the water," he shouted. "Come," said Jesus.

Peter looked straight at Jesus and stepped off the side of the boat. He was walking on the water toward Jesus. Peter was doing the impossible because he had faith to do it.

But then Peter became afraid. He felt the strong wind. He stared at the angry waves. When he took his eyes off Jesus his faith was gone and he began to sink. "Save me, Lord!"

Peter cried. At once Jesus reached out and caught Peter's hand. "Where is your faith?" Jesus asked. "Why did you doubt?" As they climbed into the boat the wind stopped. Peter knew now that with faith he could do even impossible things. Without it, what could he do?

## THINK

1. What could Peter do when he had faith in Jesus? 2. What happened when his faith left him? 3. What did you learn about faith from this story?

## LEARN

From this story, you learn that with faith you can do even impossible things.

## DO

Write the letters F A I T H. Can you make a sentence about God, using these letters as the first letters of the words. For example: Father Almighty—I Thank Him.

# A Woman with Faith

## *A Story about* FAITH

Jesus and His disciples traveled far and wide through their land. Wherever Jesus went, He told the people, the Jews, about God's Good News. "Believe in Me," Jesus said to them. That was the way people could know God and some day live with Him in heaven. Some Jews believed in Jesus, but some did not.

One day Jesus left His homeland to go to another land nearby. As He walked along the road with His disciples, a woman came and bowed down before Him. "Lord, please have mercy on me," she cried. "There is a demon in my daughter. She is in great pain."

But Jesus did not say a word to the woman. He kept walking down the road. "Tell this woman to go away," the disciples said to Jesus. "She follows us everywhere and will not leave us alone."

Finally Jesus turned around and spoke to the woman. He wanted to test her to see how much faith she had. "You are not a Jew," He said to her. "God has sent Me to help the Jews first."

But the woman would not give up. She knew that only Jesus could heal her daughter. "Please help me anyway," she pleaded. Jesus again turned to the woman. "How can I help you since you are not a Jew?" He said. "But You must help me," the woman begged. "No one else can."

"You have great faith," Jesus said to the woman. "And because you believe in Me, I will give you what you ask."

At that very moment, the woman's daughter was healed. By healing the woman's daughter, Jesus showed that He will help anyone who has faith in Him.

## THINK

1. What did the woman believe that Jesus could do? 2. Why did Jesus heal her daughter? 3. Why should we keep on praying when we want Jesus to do something for us?

## LEARN

From this story, you learn that faith is believing Jesus can do something special. When you have faith in Him, never stop praying.

## DO

Draw a clock face. Put one hand at each hour. Then write the word PRAY above it. This will remind you to pray any time of the day.

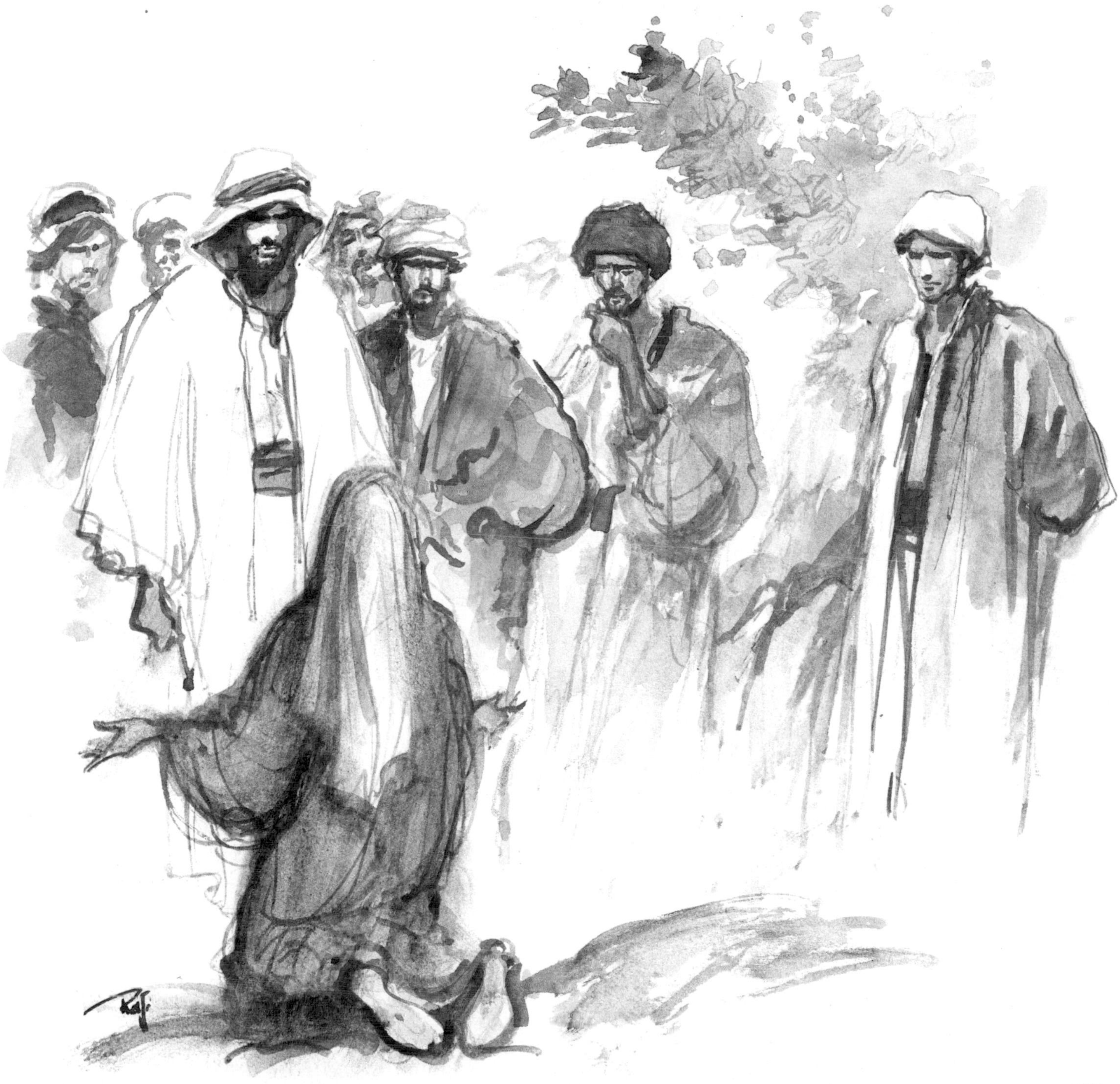

# Jesus Heals Ten Lepers

## *A Story about* THANKFULNESS

Ten men were very sick. They had leprosy. No doctor could cure them. The poor lepers had to live by themselves. They could not go into town because someone might catch their disease.

One day the lepers were sitting on a hillside outside the town. "Look!" one of them cried. "Jesus is coming to town." The lepers knew about Jesus. They had heard how He healed other lepers.

"Jesus, Master, please help us," they shouted from a distance. The men did not want to get too close because the people following Jesus were afraid of catching their leprosy. "Go and find a priest," Jesus told them. Jesus was saying that the men would be healed by the time they found a priest. Then the priest would pronounce them "clean" or healed.

The ten lepers turned and ran toward town, looking for a priest. As they ran they shouted with joy. They were not lepers anymore! But one leper stopped running. While the others hurried ahead into town, the one leper came back to thank Jesus before he did anything else.

When the man found Jesus he fell on his knees before Him. "Thank You, Jesus, for healing me," he said. "How I praise God for what you have done for me."

Then Jesus asked, "Didn't I heal ten men? Where are the others?" Jesus was pleased with the man who had returned to thank Him. "Of the ten men, you are the only one to come back and thank Me," Jesus said to him. "And because you are the most thankful, you will also be the happiest."

## THINK

1. What did the ten men want Jesus to do? 2. When He helped them, how many came back to thank Him? 3. How many times have you thanked Jesus this week?

## LEARN

From this story, you learn that you should thank Jesus when He helps you.

## DO

Before you do anything else, bow your head and thank Jesus for something special He has done for you.

# Jesus Heals a Blind Man

*A Story about* WISDOM

"Is that man blind because he sinned?" the disciples asked, pointing to the man beside the road.

Jesus looked kindly toward the poor blind man. "Sin did not make him blind," Jesus replied. "This happened so that the man will come to know God."

The blind man began to listen to Jesus. Suddenly he felt something smooth and cool on his eyes. "Go and wash your eyes in the Pool of Siloam," Jesus told him, "and you will see." The man jumped up and made his way to the pool as fast as he could. When he dipped his face in the water, the mud Jesus had put on his eyes fell off, and he saw all the things he had only imagined before.

His friends could not believe what happened so they took him to the Pharisees. "How did you receive your sight?" they asked. then the man who had been blind told them about Jesus.

The Pharisees did not like Jesus. They didn't want to believe that Jesus was the Messiah because it would make their job less important. "Give glory to God," the Pharisees demanded, "for we know that Jesus is a sinner." The Pharisees thought they were wise, but they were not.

"You know that God does not listen to sinners," the man answered. "If Jesus were not from God He could not have healed me."

The man did not know much compared to the Pharisees, but he was far wiser, for the Pharisees would not believe in Jesus and the man did. The Pharisees were more blind than he had ever been.

## THINK

1. The blind man probably never went to school, while the Pharisees went to school for a long time. How was he wiser than they were? 2. Which is more important, to know many things or to be wise about God? Why? 3. What is the wisest thing we can do? Have you accepted Jesus as your Savior?

## LEARN

From this story, you learn that wise people receive Jesus, no matter how much or how little they know.

## DO

If you have not accepted Jesus, bow your head and ask Him to be your Savior. Then tell someone you love about what you have done.

# Parable of the Good Samaritan

## A Story about LOVE

"What must I do to go to heaven?" a man asked Jesus one day. "You are a teacher of God's laws," Jesus replied. "What do you think?" Jesus said this because He knew the man was trying to trick Him.

"God's law tells us that we must first love God more than anything else," the man answered. "Then we must love our neighbor as much as we love ourselves." Jesus said to the man, "You are exactly right. Do this and you will go to heaven."

When the man saw that he could not trick Jesus, he asked Him another question, "But who is my neighbor?" he asked. "Who are the people I am supposed to love?"

Jesus answered the man by telling him a story. "Once a man was traveling to Jericho. Along the lonely road, robbers jumped on him and beat him until he almost died. Then they took his clothes and money, and left him lying by the side of the road.

"Soon a priest came by and saw the man, but he did not stop to help. Then a Levite came by and saw the man too, but he hurried on his way.

"When a Samaritan came along the road and saw the poor man, he stopped to help. He gave the man something to drink, put bandages on his wounds, and took him to an inn. "Please take care of this man," the Samaritan said to the innkeeper. "I will pay you whatever it costs to make him well."

"Which of the three was a neighbor to the man who was attacked by robbers?" Jesus asked the teacher of the law. The teacher replied, "The one who showed love to the man."

"Now do you understand who your neighbor is?" Jesus asked the teacher. "It is anyone who needs you. Go and love your neighbor, and do whatever you can to help him."

## THINK

1. What two questions did the teacher ask Jesus? 2. Jesus told the man a story. Can you tell the story the way Jesus told it? 3. What did Jesus tell the teacher to do? 4. What can you do to show someone that you love Jesus, and that you love that person, too?

## LEARN

From this story, you learn that you should show love to those around you.

## DO

Think of someone special. Now think of something you can do to show that person love. Will you do it?

143

# The Parable of the Lost Sheep

*A Story about* JOY

Some men who had done many bad things invited Jesus to dinner. Jesus ate with them and told them how to be sorry for their sins. He told them how to find God.

The Pharisees were angry when they saw Jesus with these people. The Pharisees did not like them. They thought they were better than these men who had done so many bad things. "Jesus must be a sinner too," the Pharisees said to themselves. "A good man would not eat with those bad people."

When Jesus heard the Pharisees say this, He told them a story. "There was a shepherd who had a hundred sheep. But one night, when he brought his sheep in from the fields, he counted only ninety-nine.

"The shepherd left the ninety-nine sheep, and went out to look for the one that was lost. He hunted everywhere for that one lost sheep. When he finally found it he was full of joy. Gently he put the little sheep on his shoulders and carried it home.

"The shepherd was so happy that he invited all his friends and neighbors together. He had to tell them the joy he felt because he had brought his lost sheep home."

Then Jesus said to the Pharisees, "The men who have done bad things are like the lost sheep. I came to earth to help them find God. Those who already love God, have already found Him! So there is greater joy in heaven for one lost person who finds God, than for ninety-nine who already know Him.

## THINK

1. Why were the Pharisees angry at Jesus? 2. What did the shepherd do when he brought his lost lamb safely home? 3. What brings joy in heaven?

## LEARN

From this story, you learn that there is joy in heaven when one lost person finds God.

## DO

Think of a friend who does not know Jesus. Pray for that friend each day this week. Would you like to talk with your friend after that?

# The Prodigal Son

## A Story about FORGIVENESS

Jesus loved to tell stories called parables. Jesus' parables were special, because each taught a lesson about God.

One day Jesus told some people a parable about a boy who ran away. "There was a boy who wanted to leave his home," Jesus began. "His home was big and beautiful. His parents loved him very much. But the boy thought he would have more fun away from home.

"So the boy asked his father for some money. This was the money his father was saving for a time when the boy was older. But the boy wanted all the money now.

"With the money in his pocket, the boy ran far away to another country. There he spent his money to have a good time.

"But one day all of his money was gone. Soon he became hungry. 'What shall I do?' the boy asked himself. No one would help him. Nobody cared.

"Then the boy remembered his father. He remembered his big, beautiful home. He was ashamed, but he headed home anyway.

"When the boy's father saw him, he ran down the road, threw his arms around his son and kissed him.

" 'Father, I am not good enough to be your son,' the boy said. 'Please hire me as a servant.'

" 'No,' the father said. 'You will always be my son. I love you now more than ever.'

"Now the boy was back in his beautiful home. His parents still loved him very much. And they had completely forgiven him for all the bad things he had done."

## THINK

1. Why did the boy go away from home? 2. What did he do while he was away? 3. When he finally went home, what did his father do?

## LEARN

From this story, you learn that forgiveness is not holding bad things against people, but receiving people as Jesus would.

## DO

Have you done something bad, and want to be forgiven? Will you go ask the person who should forgive you now?

# Jesus and the Children

## A Story about LOVE

Jesus had a wonderful touch. His hands made sick people well, and blind people see, and His words helped people who hurt inside. How wonderful it was to be near Jesus!

Jesus was always helping people. Crowds followed Him everywhere. One day some mothers brought their children to Jesus. They wanted Jesus to touch their children. They wanted Him to say kind words to them. The children wanted to see Jesus too.

But the disciples tried to send the mothers away. "Jesus does not have time to talk with your children," they said. "He has too many important things to do."

Jesus did not like what the disciples said. "Please bring the children to Me," He told the mothers. Jesus put His arms around the children. He asked God to bless them.

Then Jesus said to His disciples, "If you want to go to heaven, you must become like these children. God will accept you if you put away your pride and see others as better than yourself."

Jesus loves children. He loves anyone who wants to come to Him.

## THINK

1. Why did the disciples try to send the children away? 2. What did Jesus do then? 3. What did Jesus say the disciples had to do before they could get to heaven?

## LEARN

From this story, you learn that Jesus loves children, and anyone else who wants to come to Him.

## DO

Cut out several pictures of children from magazines and paste them together on a sheet of paper. Hang this in your room to remind you that Jesus loves children.

# Jesus Raises Lazarus

*A Story about* FAITH

When Lazarus became sick, his sisters, Mary and Martha, were worried. "Run and tell Jesus that His friend Lazarus is about to die," they told someone.

But Jesus was far away. It took Him many days to come to Mary and Martha's house, so by that time Lazarus was dead. When Martha heard that Jesus was coming, she ran down the road to meet Him. "If only You had been here, I know that Lazarus would not have died," she said to Him.

"Do you believe in Me?" Jesus asked Martha. "I believe that You are God's Son, and that God will do whatever You ask," she answered. "Good," Jesus said. "Keep believing and you will see wonderful things."

Then Mary came running down the road. Others followed, crying. "If only You had been here, Lazarus would not have died," she said to Jesus.

Jesus looked at Mary and Martha. They were crying. All of the people with them were crying too. Then Jesus cried. He loved Mary, Martha and Lazarus. They were such good friends.

"Please take Me to the cave where Lazarus is buried," Jesus asked. When they reached the cave, Jesus said to some men, "Roll away the stone that covers the cave entrance."

"But Lazarus has been dead four days," Martha said to Jesus. "You don't really want to go inside."

Jesus then said to Martha, "Didn't I tell you that if you believe, you will see wonderful things?"

The men rolled the stone away from the cave. "Lazarus, come out!" Jesus shouted in a loud voice. Lazarus came out of the cave, still wrapped in his grave clothes. He was alive!

Mary and Martha were full of joy. They were glad that they believed in Jesus. Now they believed in Jesus even more.

## THINK

1. Why did Mary and Martha send for Jesus when Lazarus was sick? 2. What did Jesus ask Martha to do? 3. What do you do when you need help? 4. Do you believe that Jesus can help you when you need Him?

## LEARN

From this story, you learn that believing in Jesus is believing that He can do anything.

## DO

John 11:25 is a good verse to memorize. Would you like to do that?

# Zacchaeus Is Forgiven

## *A Story about* FORGIVENESS

Zacchaeus thought he had everything he wanted. He had money, a good job, and he lived in a big house with many servants. But Zacchaeus was not happy, because he cheated people to get his money.

Zacchaeus was a tax collector. When it was time to pay taxes, Zacchaeus made the people pay more money than they should. This made Zacchaeus rich. But it also made him unhappy.

One day Jesus came to town. Zacchaeus wanted to see Jesus. But many other people wanted to see Jesus too. Before Zacchaeus could find Jesus, there was a big crowd around Him. Zacchaeus was too short to see over the crowd, so he climbed a sycamore tree by the side of the road. Now he could see Jesus coming.

Suddenly Jesus stopped under the tree where Zacchaeus was waiting. "Zacchaeus," said Jesus, "climb down from that tree. I want to come to your house today."

Zacchaeus was surprised. When he got home, he made a big dinner for Jesus. Then he told Jesus how sorry he was for all the bad things he had done. "I will pay back all the money I have taken from the people," Zacchaeus promised.

Jesus saw that Zacchaeus was sorry for his sins. "Today God has forgiven you," Jesus said. Now Zacchaeus was happy, because he really did have everything he wanted.

## THINK

1. How did Zacchaeus get rich? 2. Why wasn't he happy when he had so much? 3. What did Zacchaeus tell Jesus? 4. Why did that make him happy?

## LEARN

From this story, you learn that you are happier when someone forgives you for wrong things you have done. You are happier also when you forgive someone for something wrong.

## DO

Which of the following do you do when you forgive someone? (1) Hold a grudge against them. (2) Stay angry at them. (3) Pretend they never did something wrong. (4) Forget what they did wrong.

# Jesus Rides Into Jerusalem

*A Story about* PRAISE

The air was filled with excitement as Jesus and His disciples walked down the Mount of Olives toward Jerusalem. Crowds swarmed around Him, for they thought Jesus would crown Himself king of Israel when He arrived in the city. But Jesus wanted to be king of their lives, not their country.

"Go to the town ahead of us," Jesus told two of His disciples. "There you will find a donkey tied to a post. Untie him and bring him back to Me." The disciples did what Jesus asked. They found the donkey and brought him back to Jesus. Then the disciples put their coats on the donkey's back, and Jesus sat on the donkey.

Many people took off their coats and laid them on the road before Jesus. "Jesus is our king!" they shouted. "Praise God for sending Jesus to bring peace to the earth."

As Jesus neared Jerusalem, more people ran to meet Him. They cut palm branches from the trees and laid them on the road. The people began to sing and praise God. "Hosanna! Hosanna to our king," they shouted.

The people were very happy as they watched Jesus enter Jerusalem. They sang and shouted for joy. The Pharisees tried to quiet the crowd. But Jesus said to them, "If the people are quiet, then the stones will speak up and praise God." So there was great joy in Jerusalem that day as the people praised God that Jesus, their king, had come.

## THINK

1. Why were the people happy to see Jesus? 2. What did the people do when Jesus rode into Jerusalem? 3. How did the people praise God? 4. Why should we praise God?

## LEARN

From this story, you learn to praise God. This means you should thank God for sending Jesus, and for all the other wonderful things He does for you.

## DO

Think of two things for which you should praise God. Will you pray now and thank Him for them?

# Parable of Wise and Foolish Girls

## *A Story about* RESPONSIBILITY

"Soon I am going to heaven," Jesus told His disciples one day. "But some day I will come back."

"Please tell us when You are coming back," His disciples asked. "We want to be ready for You." But Jesus said, "Only God knows when I will return. So you must always watch and be ready."

Then Jesus told them a parable. "Ten girls came to a wedding one night. Each girl carried a little oil lamp to light her way through the dark streets.

"The ten girls waited a long time for the bridegroom to arrive. Soon they fell asleep. Five of the girls were wise, so they brought extra oil for their lamps. The other five were foolish. They did not take extra oil for their lamps.

"At last the bridegroom came. The ten girls jumped up to greet him. The five wise girls put the extra oil in their lamps and they burned brightly. They were ready for the bridegroom.

"But the five foolish girls were not ready. While they were sleeping, their lamps had burned all their oil. These girls ran to buy more oil for their lamps, but when they returned, it was too late. They could not get in to the wedding because the bridegroom's doors were already locked. They were sorry that they were not prepared."

Then Jesus said to His disciples, "You must be like the five wise girls. Always be ready, because you do not know when I will come back." That is a good way to show responsibility, isn't it?

## THINK

1. What did the five wise girls do to stay ready for the bridegroom? 2. Why were the five foolish girls not ready? 3. Jesus is coming again someday. What should you do to stay ready for Him?

## LEARN

From this story, you learn about responsibility. When you are responsible, you are ready to do the things you are supposed to.

## DO

Talk with your parents or a teacher about responsibility. Ask them how they think you should show responsibility at home, Sunday school, or school.

# The Last Supper

## *A Story about* REMEMBERING

"Go into Jerusalem," Jesus told Peter and John. "Find a room where we can eat the Passover meal together." "But where shall we look?" the two disciples asked. "When you enter the city," Jesus answered, "you will see a man carrying a jug of water. Follow him to his house, and ask him if he has an extra room. He will show you the room."

The disciples obeyed Jesus. Everything happened the way Jesus said. Soon Jesus and His disciples were in the upstairs room where they sat down at the table together.

But Jesus was sad. "One of you is about to betray Me," He said, looking at Judas. Just before supper Judas had been paid thirty pieces of silver to betray Jesus. Now Judas felt ashamed and left the room, for he was sure that Jesus knew what he was doing.

Jesus stayed with the eleven disciples who were faithful to Him. He took some bread and broke it into little pieces. Then He thanked God for the bread. "Eat some of this bread," Jesus said to each of His disciples. "Do this often when I am no longer with you. It will help you remember Me."

Then Jesus poured some wine into a cup and thanked God for it. "Drink some of this," Jesus said to each of His disciples. "Do this often when I am no longer with you. It will help you remember Me."

Just before they left to go outside, Jesus told the disciples He was going away. The disciples thought Jesus was going on a long trip, but Jesus knew He was going to die. Once again Jesus reminded them, "Get together often to do these things. Then you will remember Me until I come back again."

## THINK

1. How did Jesus ask His disciples to remember Him? 2. Why is it important for us to remember Jesus every day? 3. What can you do to remember Jesus every day?

## LEARN

From this story, you learn what Jesus has done for you. When you remember all Jesus has done for you, you will love Him. When you love Jesus you want to obey Him.

## DO

Find a picture of Jesus in some Sunday school papers you have brought home. Cut it out and paste it on a sheet of paper. Write REMEMBER under it. Hang it in your room, and it will help you remember Jesus this week.

# Judas Betrays Jesus

## A Story about FAITHFULNESS

It was night in Jerusalem when Jesus and His disciples left the upstairs room where they had eaten supper. They made their way through the dark streets, out the city gate, to a quiet garden on the Mount of Olives.

In the garden Jesus prayed until men with flickering torches came from the city. The disciples jumped up. Soon they saw soldiers carrying the torches and Judas was leading them.

Judas walked up to Jesus and kissed Him. He had been paid to do this to show the soldiers which one was Jesus.

But the soldiers were afraid of Jesus, for they had heard of the things He had done. Finally some of them stepped forward to take hold of Jesus. Peter angrily took his sword and cut off one man's ear.

"Put away your sword, Peter," Jesus told him. "Don't you know that I could call ten thousand angels to rescue Me?" Jesus healed the man's ear. Then the soldiers took Jesus away.

Back in the city, Judas began to think how unfaithful he had been to Jesus. The money did not make Judas happy. Finally he went back to the men who had given it to him. "Take back your money," Judas said. "Jesus has done nothing wrong."

But the men would not take back the money. They knew Jesus had done nothing wrong. But they still wanted to kill Him. Judas threw the money on the floor and ran out. Then Judas felt so sorry because he had been unfaithful that he killed himself. How sad that Judas never learned to be faithful to Jesus, for that is what makes us truly happy.

### THINK

1. Why did Judas betray Jesus to the evil men? 2. Why did Judas think that would make him happy? 3. Why do you think Judas killed himself?

### LEARN

From this story, you learn that faithfulness makes us happy, and unfaithfulness makes us unhappy.

### DO

Just before the story of Judas betraying Jesus, there is a parable about faithfulness. You may wish to read it in Matthew 25:14-30. Count the number of times the word faithful appears.

# Jesus Is Crucified

*A Story about* FORGIVENESS

"This man must die," Jesus' enemies said to Pilate, the governor. "What has He done wrong?" Pilate asked. But the men could not think of one thing that Jesus had done wrong. Pilate asked Jesus many questions. But he could find nothing wrong. Then he said to the men, "I will let Him go."

"No! He must die!" the men shouted. Then they stirred up people to shout with them. Pilate was afraid of the people. Finally he sent Jesus away to die.

Pilate's soldiers took Jesus away, put a crown of thorns on His head, and hit Him until He was hurt and bleeding. But Jesus said nothing bad to the men. He still loved them and forgave them because they did not know He was God's Son.

At last the soldiers made Jesus drag a heavy wooden cross through the streets to a hill outside the city. Then they nailed Jesus on the cross, pounding nails through His hands and feet, and left Him there to die.

Jesus' friends and disciples were weeping at the foot of the cross. They did not understand why Jesus had to die. Beside them the soldiers threw dice to see who would get Jesus' clothes.

At noon the sky turned black. God covered up the sun for three hours. Then the ground shook and great rocks split into pieces. Jesus cried out to God, "Father forgive them. They do not know what they are doing." Then Jesus died. His work was finished. Jesus had paid for the sins of the world.

God had kept His greatest promise. Because Jesus died, God will forgive the sins of every man and woman who comes to Him. How wonderful that we can be forgiven!

## THINK

1. What did Jesus' enemies want to do to Him?
2. What had Jesus done wrong? 3. What did Jesus say about the men who wanted to kill Him? 4. What should we do about people who want to hurt us?

## LEARN

From this story, you learn that Jesus will forgive us for all the bad things we have done. Shouldn't we forgive others when they do something bad to us?

## DO

Do you need to forgive someone? Will you do it now?

# Jesus Is Risen

*A Story about* FAITH

Early one morning some women made their way to Jesus' tomb. When they reached the tomb they saw that the stone covering the entrance was rolled away. One of the women, Mary Magdalene, cried out, "Someone has taken Jesus away." Mary turned and ran back to Jerusalem.

The other women went ahead to look into the tomb. There was an angel! "Don't be afraid," said the angel. "I know you are looking for Jesus. But He is not here. He is risen! Don't you remember that Jesus promised you He would rise three days after His death?"

The women remembered now what Jesus had promised. They wanted to tell the rest of the disciples that Jesus was alive. "We should have believed what Jesus told us," they said as they ran back to Jerusalem.

Mary Magdalene was already in Jerusalem. At last she found Peter and John. "Someone has stolen Jesus' body," she said to them. Mary had not yet seen the angel, so she did not know Jesus had risen. Peter and John ran to the tomb and looked inside. It was empty. "Don't you see?" John said to Peter. "Jesus is alive!" Then the two disciples went back to Jerusalem.

Mary sat down beside the empty tomb and began to cry. "Why are you crying?" someone asked her. "Who are you looking for?" Mary looked up at the man. She thought he was the gardener. "Did you take Jesus away?" she asked.

"Mary, don't you know who I am?" He asked. Then Mary saw that it was Jesus. Mary was so happy. Now she knew that Jesus was God's Son. Jesus did die to forgive her sins. "I believe in Jesus," she said as she ran to Jerusalem to tell the disciples the happy news.

## THINK

1. What did the women find when they came to the tomb? 2. What had happened? 3. Why should we be happy that Jesus rose from the dead?

## LEARN

From this story, you learn to have faith that when Jesus promises something, He will do it!

## DO

Look at the picture on the opposite page. Do you see the large round stone? Stones like these were rolled across the tomb opening to keep people out.

# On the Way to Emmaus

## *A Story about* FAITH

Two disciples were walking home on the road to Emmaus. "Did Jesus really rise from the dead?" they wondered. "Or did someone steal His body to make it look like He rose from the dead?"

As they talked about these things, a man came along and walked with them. "What are you talking about?" the man asked. "Haven't you heard what has happened in Jerusalem?" they answered.

Then the disciples told the man about Jesus. "He was a great prophet," they said. "We thought He would be our king and rule Israel. But men nailed him to a cross and he died."

"What else happened?" the man asked. "It has been three days since Jesus died," the disciples said. "This morning some of our friends went to His tomb but found it empty. They said some angels were at the tomb. The angels told them Jesus had risen!"

Then the man said to the disciples, "Why does it take you so long to have faith in the promises of God's Word? Haven't you read that Jesus had to die, but after three days He would live again?"

After that, the man told the disciples many wonderful things from God's Word. The disciples were amazed as they listened to him.

At last they arrived in Emmaus. "Please stay and eat with us," the disciples asked the man. As they sat at the table, the man took bread and thanked God for it. Suddenly the disciples knew who the man was. He was Jesus! But just then Jesus disappeared.

The disciples knew now what God's Word said about Jesus. Never again would they doubt God's Word.

## THINK

1. What did Jesus say to the two men when He walked with them on the road? 2. When did they recognize that the man was Jesus? 3. What did the men learn about faith in God's Word? 4. What did you learn about faith in God's Word?

## LEARN

From this story, you learn that you should have faith in God's Word, believing what it says.

## DO

Talk about these three questions with your parents or teacher: (1) Who wrote God's Word? (2) Why should we believe it? (3) What will we do to share it with others?

# The Disciples Go Fishing Again

## A Story about FAITH

"Jesus is alive!" said the two disciples from Emmaus. They ran all the way back to Jerusalem to tell the others.

"We have seen Jesus!" they said. As they were talking, Jesus suddenly stood before them. The disciples were afraid. The door was locked, but Jesus was in the room. Was this a ghost?

"Why do you still have doubts?" Jesus asked them. "Look at the scars in My hands and side." The disciples shouted for joy. It really was Jesus. "Now we truly believe You are God's Son," they said.

Several nights later the disciples went fishing on the Sea of Galilee. All night they threw their nets into the water, but caught nothing. When morning came, they gave up, and sailed their boat toward shore.

The disciples saw a man standing on the shore. "Did you catch any fish?" the man asked. "No," they answered. "Then throw your net on the other side of the boat," the man told them.

The disciples did what the man told them. At once the net was so full of fish it started to break. "That man must be Jesus," John said to Peter.

Peter couldn't wait to see Jesus. He jumped from the boat and ran through the water to greet Him. The other disciples brought the boat to shore, dragging the net full of fish behind.

Jesus talked with the disciples all day. He taught them how to follow Him. Then he told them how to teach others to follow Him. Some of the disciples wrote books about the wonderful things Jesus did on earth. These books are now part of our Bible. The disciples wrote these books so that we too might have faith in Jesus. Do you believe in Him?

## THINK

1. What happened when Jesus appeared to the disciples in the room? 2. What did Jesus show them to help them believe He had risen? 3. Why can we believe that Jesus has risen? How do you know?

## LEARN

From this story, you learn that you can have faith that Jesus rose from the dead. When you believe in Jesus, He forgives all your sins.

## DO

Which of these words tell about faith? Which do not? BELIEVE, DOUBT, ACCEPT, REJECT.

# Jesus Ascends Into Heaven

## A Story about PROMISES

It was time for Jesus to go back to his home in heaven. He had spent many days with His disciples after He had risen. He had taught them many important things, especially to believe in God's promises.

"Long, long ago, God promised to send His Son to you," Jesus told them. "I have come, so God has kept His promise. Then God promised that I would die to save you from sin, and that I would rise again. He has kept that promise too."

One day Jesus took His disciples to the top of a hill near Jerusalem. "God has another wonderful promise for you," Jesus told them. "Soon He will send His Holy Spirit to live in your hearts. The Holy Spirit will help you while I am in heaven."

"You must return to Jerusalem and wait for God to send you the Holy Spirit," Jesus said. "Then you must go throughout the world, telling people that I can save them from their sins."

As Jesus was talking to the disciples, He suddenly began to rise. "I promise to return some day," He said to them. Then Jesus went higher and higher into the sky. Soon He was gone.

As the disciples stared into the sky, two angels appeared beside them. "Why do you look into the sky?" they asked. "Jesus is in heaven. But someday He will come again, just as He promised."

The disciples walked back to Jerusalem. They were happy that Jesus was in heaven, watching over them. they stayed in the city, waiting for the Holy Spirit. They knew that God keeps all His promises. And they knew that someday God would keep His greatest promise—Jesus would return!

## THINK

1. What had God promised about His Son? 2. Did He keep His promise? 3. What did He promise about the Holy Spirit? 4. How do you know that you can trust God to keep His promises?

## LEARN

From this story, you learn that God always keeps His promises. We should keep ours, too.

## DO

If one of your parents or teachers wears a wedding ring, ask what that ring means. You will learn something about promises.

# God Sends His Holy Spirit

## *A Story about* COURAGE

After Jesus went back to heaven, the disciples waited in Jerusalem for the Holy Spirit to come. Each day they met together in a house to pray. One day they heard a loud rushing noise like a great wind. Then little flames of fire stood over each one of them.

Suddenly the disciples began to speak in foreign languages. The Holy Spirit had come into their hearts, and helped them speak languages they did not know. Now they wanted to tell everyone about Jesus. They were not afraid, for the Holy Spirit had given them courage.

At that time, Jews had come from all over the world to attend a great feast in Jerusalem. When they heard the loud rushing noise, they ran to the house to see what was happening.

When these visitors listened to the disciples speak their languages, they were excited. "Something wonderful is happening here," they said. But some of them made fun of the disciples.

Peter stood up and talked to the crowd. "You are seeing the power of the Holy Spirit at work," he said. Then Peter told the people about Jesus. "You killed Jesus, God's Son," Peter said. "But He is alive! We saw Him before He went back to heaven. Now He has sent His Holy spirit to help us."

The people were afraid. "We did not know Jesus was God's Son," they said. "We are sorry we did that to Him. "What can we do now?"

"Believe that Jesus is God's Son," Peter told them. "He can save you from your sins." Many of them did believe. The Holy Spirit came into their hearts too. Then God gave them courage to tell others about Jesus, just as He had given the disciples courage.

## THINK

1. Why were the disciples waiting in Jerusalem? 2. How did the Holy Spirit come to the disciples? 3. How did the Holy Spirit help the disciples tell others about Jesus?

## LEARN

From this story, you learn that the Holy Spirit gives us courage to tell others about Jesus.

## DO

Ask God to give you courage, through the Holy Spirit, to tell your friends about Jesus.

# Stephen Dies for Jesus

## *A Story about* FORGIVENESS

The disciples were too busy! They needed help! So they chose seven men to work with them, teaching people about Jesus and bringing food to the poor. The Holy Spirit helped Stephen, one of these seven men, do many wonderful miracles for the people.

But there were some men who hated Stephen. These were the same men who hated Jesus. "We must do something about him," they said. "He is helping too many people believe in Jesus."

So the wicked men brought Stephen to the high priest and told lies about him. "We heard this man say things against God," they said. "Is it true?" the high priest asked Stephen. "Are you saying bad things about God?"

Stephen was not afraid. The Holy Spirit made him brave. Suddenly Stephen's face began to shine like the face of an angel. Then Stephen told the high priest about Jesus. "I see the gates of heaven opening," Stephen said. "And I see Jesus standing next to God."

But the high priest and his men did not want to listen to Stephen. They wanted to hurt him. When the men heard Stephen say this they dragged him from the city and threw stones at him.

Stephen got on his knees to pray. "Please forgive these men," he prayed. That was what Jesus prayed on the cross. The men threw stones at Stephen until he died. But Stephen was not afraid. He knew that he would soon go to live with Jesus.

### THINK

1. What kind of man was Stephen? 2. What did Stephen say about the men who threw stones at him? 3. Why did he forgive them? 4. Why should we forgive others who hurt us?

### LEARN

From this story, you learn that you should forgive others who say bad things about you, or try to hurt you.

### DO

Find a stone and bring it to your dinner table tonight. Talk with your family about Stephen. Talk about how this stone can remind you to forgive others.

174

# Philip and the Ethiopian

## A Story about LISTENING

Philip was a busy man, preaching to the people of Samaria, telling them about Jesus, and doing a miracle here and there. What an exciting life as hundreds of people listened to Philip tell about Jesus.

Then God sent an angel to Philip. "Go to the road that leads to Gaza," the angel told him. Philip obeyed the angel and left the crowds at Samaria. He must have wondered what God wanted him to do in that lonely place.

As Philip walked along the road, he saw a beautiful chariot pulled by horses. The chariot came nearer and Philip saw an Ethiopian official. The man was reading God's Word.

"Do you understand what you are reading?" Philip asked him. The Ethiopian shook his head. "I need someone to help me. Do you understand this book?"

When Philip stepped into the chariot, he looked at the book. It was something the prophet Isaiah had written about Jesus hundreds of years before. "Who is the prophet Isaiah talking about?" asked the Ethiopian.

"Isaiah was telling us that someday Jesus would come," Philip told him. "And now He has come! He died for our sins." Then Philip told the Ethiopian about Jesus. The man listened carefully.

"I believe in Jesus," the Ethiopian said to Philip. So they got out of the chariot and found some water by the side of the road. There Philip baptized the Ethiopian. Suddenly Philip was gone. God had taken him away where someone else could listen to him tell about Jesus. The Ethiopian went home happy. Now he wanted to tell others who would listen to him tell about Jesus too.

## THINK

1. Why did God send Philip to the Gaza road? 2. What did the Ethiopian ask Philip to do? What did Philip tell the Ethiopian? 3. Why should we want to listen when others tell about Jesus? 4. Why do you hope others will listen when you tell them about Jesus?

## LEARN

From this story, you learn that it is good to listen when others tell about Jesus.

## DO

Ask someone to talk to you. While they are talking, put your fingers in your ears. What do you hear? Suppose that person is saying something important. Will you hear it? What do you learn when you do not listen?

# Peter Is Thrown Into Prison

## A Story about PRAYER

Things were not easy for the believers in Jerusalem. Many of their neighbors hated anyone who believed in Jesus.

One day King Herod wanted to make these enemies of Jesus happy. "Find James, the disciple of Jesus," Herod told his soldiers. Then Herod killed James, which made those evil people happy.

When Herod saw that he had pleased these people, he said to his soldiers, "Bring Peter, another disciple of Jesus." Herod threw Peter into prison. He ordered two soldiers to guard the heavy iron gate. Then he chained Peter to other soldiers inside the prison.

"Tomorrow I will kill Peter," Herod said. When the believers heard this, they met at John Mark's house, and prayed for Peter. They asked God to take care of him.

In the middle of the night, while Peter and the soldiers were fast asleep, God sent an angel to the prison. The angel's shining face lit up the dark prison as the angel shook Peter.

Peter opened his eyes and looked at the angel. "I must be dreaming," he thought. "Get up!" the angel said to Peter. "Put on your coat and follow me." When Peter stood up, the chains fell off his hands and feet.

Peter followed the angel out of the prison, but the soldiers did not see them. When they came to the large iron gate, it opened up for them, and Peter and the angel walked past the soldiers. Suddenly the angel was gone.

Peter could hardly believe it. Was this a dream? But there he was, standing outside the prison. "God really did send an angel to save me," Peter said.

Peter ran down the streets to John Mark's house and knocked on the courtyard gate. Inside, his friends were still praying for him. A girl named Rhoda came to the gate to see who was knocking.

When she heard Peter's voice, she was so excited she ran to tell the others, and left Peter outside. "Peter is knocking at the gate," Rhoda told the believers. "That is impossible," they said. "Peter is in prison."

But Peter kept knocking. At last someone went to open the gate. There was Peter! How happy they were! Then Peter told them how the angel had freed him from prison.

The believers were glad they had prayed for Peter. "God does answer our prayers," they said.

## THINK

1. Why did Herod put Peter in prison? 2. What did the believers do to help Peter? 3. How did Peter get out of prison? 4. What can God do for you when you pray?

## LEARN

From this story, you learn that it is never too late to pray for God's help.

## DO

1 Corinthians 5:17 is a good verse about prayer. Would you like to memorize it?

# Jesus Talks With Saul

## *A Story about* FORGIVENESS

Saul was on his way to Damascus. "What are we going to do?" asked the believers who lived there. They knew Saul would throw them into prison or hurt them because they loved Jesus.

Saul lived in Jerusalem. He was a religious leader, but he hated Jesus. He did not believe Jesus was God's Son. Saul had hurt many believers in Jerusalem and sent some to prison.

Now Saul was going to Damascus to hurt the believers there too. When the high priest had told Saul he could do this, he left with some other men.

Saul and his men went down the road toward Damascus. After several days, when they were almost there, a bright light suddenly shined down from heaven. It was so bright Saul fell to the ground. "Saul! Saul!" a voice called. "Why are you hurting Me?"

"Who is speaking to me?" Saul asked. The voice answered, "I am Jesus." Saul was afraid, for now he knew that Jesus was God's Son. He was sorry that he had been hurting Jesus' friends. "What must I do?" he asked Jesus.

"Go into Damascus and I will show you what to do," Jesus said. Then the light was gone. Saul opened his eyes, but he couldn't see, for the light had made him blind. Saul staggered to his feet and his men helped him into Damascus. There he waited to see what Jesus would do.

While Saul waited, Jesus told Ananias, a believer in Damascus, to find him. When Ananias put his hands on Saul, God let him see again. Saul asked Ananias to tell him more about Jesus. Saul was sure now that Jesus had forgiven him for all the bad things he had done.

## THINK

1. Why did Saul want to hurt the believers? 2. What did Jesus do to stop him? 3. What makes you think that Jesus forgave Saul?

## LEARN

From this story, you learn that Jesus forgives people who are truly sorry for their sins.

## DO

Have you asked Jesus to forgive you and take away your sins? If not, would you like to do that now?

# Paul Becomes a Missionary

*A Story about* DEDICATION

The good news about Jesus was spreading everywhere. Soon there were many who believed in Him. These believers, who were now called Christians, started churches, places where they could meet together to worship.

Saul and Barnabas were with a church in the town of Antioch. One day, when the Christians there met to pray, the Holy Spirit said, "I have a special job for Saul and Barnabas. I want them to travel to faraway lands, and tell people there about Jesus.

God showed Saul and Barnabas where to go on their journey. When the Antioch church dedicated them to the Lord, they boarded a large ship and sailed away on the Great Sea. "We will go wherever God wants us to," they said. After this, Saul was called Paul.

Paul and Barnabas traveled first to the island of Cyprus, where they helped the governor to believe in Jesus. Then they went to many cities in Asia. It was a long journey. They healed the sick, and helped a lame man to walk. They helped the Christians in many of the cities to start their own churches.

But there was trouble along the way. Some people chased them out of their cities. Others threw stones at them to kill them.

Paul and Barnabas tried not to be discouraged. Wherever they went, they did their best to tell others about Jesus. More than anything else, they wanted to please Him. After a long time, Paul and Barnabas came home and told the church about the wonderful things that had happened. Paul and Barnabas were happy that the news of Jesus was spreading around the world. They were doing their best for Jesus as good missionaries. That's what dedicated Christians try to do, isn't it?

## THINK

1. Where did Paul and Barnabas go? 2. What did they do? 3. Why did they want to do their best for Jesus? 4. Why should you want to do your best for Jesus?

## LEARN

From this story, you learn that dedication is doing your best for Jesus. That's what Paul and Barnabas tried to do.

## DO

Think of three things that Jesus wants you to do. Will you try to do your best in each of them today?

# Paul and Silas in Prison

*A Story about* JOY

Once again Paul got on a ship and sailed for faraway places. This time he took his friend Silas along.

One day Paul and Silas were going to be with some friends in Philippi. Along the way Paul saw a little slave girl who had an evil spirit in her. Some men owned this girl and charged people to hear what the evil spirit said.

Paul felt sorry for the little slave girl and ordered the evil spirit out of her. This made the men who owned her angry, because they couldn't make money from her any more. So these men accused Paul and Silas of doing something wrong and had them put into prison.

Paul and Silas had chains around their hands and wooden stocks around their feet, but they were filled with joy because they knew God was with them. When night came, Paul and Silas prayed and sang to God in the dark prison. They told the other prisoners about Jesus.

Suddenly the ground shook with a great earthquake. The prison doors flew open, and the chains fell off the prisoners' hands and feet.

The frightened jailor grabbed a lamp, ran through the broken prison doors, and looked down the stone steps into the prison. He knew he would be killed if the prisoners had escaped. Then he heard Paul's voice call out below, "It is all right. Everyone is here!" The jailor knew now that God had sent the earthquake. So he ran to Paul and asked, "What must I do to be saved?"

"Believe in Jesus, and you will be saved," Paul answered. When the jailor believed, joy filled his heart, too. Now he understood why Paul and Silas were so happy, even though they were in prison. Pleasing Jesus gives us joy, no matter where we are.

## THINK

1. Why were Paul and Silas put into prison? 2. What did they do while they were there? 3. Why didn't they complain to God? 4. What happened to the jailor? 5. When should you show joy in your life?

184

## LEARN

From this story, you learn to be joyful, even when things seem wrong. When we believe in Jesus, we have a reason to be joyful, because He is with us.

## DO

If you have some Bible maps at home or at Sunday School, ask someone to show you where Philippi and Jerusalem were located. Paul was far from home, wasn't he?

# Paul Is Arrested at the Temple

*A Story about* COURAGE

The Christians were glad to see Paul back home in Jerusalem. They were glad to hear him tell about new churches in faraway lands, and how God had taken care of him.

When Paul went to the temple to worship, some men who hated Jesus saw him and began to hit him. They wanted to kill Paul, but Roman soldiers took Paul away and put him in prison.

God told Paul not to worry. "You will even go to Rome," God told him. "I want the people there to know about Jesus too."

One day some men plotted to kill Paul, but Paul's nephew heard their plan and told some soldiers about it. Late that night, the soldiers took Paul away to a prison in Caesarea. There Felix, the governor, kept Paul in prison. When he called for Paul, God gave Paul courage to tell Felix about Jesus. After two years, Felix had to leave, and Festus became the new governor.

God gave Paul courage to tell Festus about Jesus, too. But Festus wanted to please the men who hated Paul, so he tried to send Paul back to Jerusalem. "If I go back to Jerusalem," said Paul, "I will be killed. I want to see Caesar." So the governor decided to send him to Caesar, the emperor who lived in Rome.

At last Paul was going to Rome, just as God had promised.

Before Paul left, a king named Agrippa came to see him. Once again God gave Paul courage to tell King Agrippa the story of Jesus.

Even while Paul was sailing for Rome, he had the courage to talk about Jesus. Because of Paul's courage, many people learned that Jesus wanted to be their Savior.

## THINK

1. Why did some men want to kill Paul? 2. Did Paul ever stop telling others about Jesus because he was afraid? 3. Why wasn't he afraid? 4. Why should you not be afraid to tell others about Jesus?

## LEARN

From this story, you learn that God gives you the courage to tell others about Jesus. Ask Him!

## DO

Would you like to ask God for special courage to do something for Him?

# Paul Is Shipwrecked

*A Story about* FAITHFULNESS

Many people would feel sorry for themselves if they had been Paul. He was a prisoner, on his way to Rome in a large sailing ship. But he was still faithfully telling people wherever he went about Jesus.

After many days, the ship was far out into the Great Sea when a storm came up. The wind blew and waves rolled over the sides of the ship.

As the storm grew worse, the sailors were sure that their ship would break apart and they would all drown. Paul could have worried about this too, but he didn't. Instead, he faithfully trusted the Lord, and helped others do that too.

"You must not be afraid," Paul told the sailors. "Last night an angel visited me and told me that none of us would die." The storm kept on, day after day, until at last the sailors found that they were coming near land. The storm was so bad that they could not steer the ship and it ran aground and began to break apart. But every man was able to swim to shore on this island and were safe. God had kept His promise.

Even on this island, Paul was faithful in telling people about Jesus, healing and helping many. When it was time to leave on another ship, Paul saw that the people were sorry to see him go.

Paul did get to Rome after another long trip, and was kept under arrest in his own house, guarded by soldiers. But even there he faithfully kept on telling people about Jesus. No matter what happened to him in any place, he never forgot to be faithful.

## THINK

1. Why do you think Paul was always faithful in telling people about Jesus? 2. Why should we always be faithful in telling others about Jesus too? 3. How does this please Jesus?

## LEARN

From this story, you learn that no matter how hard it is, you should always be faithful in telling others about Jesus.

## DO

Which of these words tell about faithfulness? LOYAL, DISLOYAL, DEVOTED, TRUE, TRUSTED, UNTRUTHFUL.

# John Writes a Special Book

## A Story about PROMISES

John had faithfully lived for Jesus all his life. Now that he was old, he was alone on an island. Some men who hated Jesus sent John here. They thought he could not tell others about Jesus on this island. But they were wrong.

One day John was sitting by the sea. Suddenly he heard a voice behind him, which sounded something like a trumpet. When John turned, he saw Jesus.

But Jesus looked so different now. His face shined so brightly that John could hardly look. John fell on his knees and covered his face. "Do not be afraid," Jesus said. "I want you to write in a book the things you are about to see."

A book was a wonderful way to tell others what Jesus would say. It was so wonderful that it is in your Bible. It is called Revelation and is the last book of the Bible.

"I promise to come back to earth some day," Jesus said. "Those who believe in Me will come to live with Me in heaven."

Then Jesus told John many wonderful things that would happen in the future. He showed John the beauty of His home in heaven, where there is no sickness, no sadness, and no night.

"I am coming back some day," Jesus said again. John believed Jesus' promise. He knew that Jesus always keeps His promises.

Today, we are just as sure that Jesus keeps His promises. We are just as sure that He will come back to earth. That is something wonderful to believe, isn't it? It is wonderful to know too that those of us who love Jesus will live forever with Him in His beautiful home in heaven.

### THINK

1. Why was John sent away to a lonely island? 2. What did Jesus tell him here? 3. Why is this important to you and me? 4. Why would you like to live in Jesus' beautiful home in heaven?

### LEARN

From this story, you learn that Jesus keeps His promises. We can be sure then that He will come back to earth some day and that we will go to live with Him in His home in heaven.

### DO

If you have not yet asked Jesus to be your Savior, would you like to do that now?

# IMPORTANT VALUES TAUGHT IN THIS BOOK

COMPASSION, Stories 57, 58
COURAGE, Stories 27, 44, 46, 82, 89
DECISION, Story 32
DEDICATION, Stories 25, 87
FAITH, Stories 55, 59, 63, 64, 72, 78, 79, 80
FAITHFULNESS, Stories 13, 29, 76, 90
FOLLOWING, Story 52
FORGIVENESS, Stories 15, 69, 72, 77, 83, 86
HAPPINESS, Story 2
HONESTY, Story 10
HUMILITY, Stories 14, 40, 51
JEALOUSY, Stories 4, 12
JOY, Stories 36, 48, 68, 88
KINDNESS, Stories 24, 39
LISTENING, Stories 60, 84
LOVE, Stories 11, 30, 67, 70
LOYALTY, Story 35
OBEDIENCE, Stories 5, 7, 17, 19, 22, 26, 41, 53, 56
ORDERLINESS, Story 1
POWER, Story 18
PRAISE, Story 73
PRAYER, Stories 43, 45, 85
PROMISES, Stories 6, 42, 47, 81, 91
PROVIDING, Stories 8, 16, 21, 38, 62
REMEMBERING, Story 75
RESPONSIBILITY, Story 74
REVERENCE, Stories 32, 49, 54
SELF-CONTROL, Story 28
TEMPTATION, Story 3
THANKFULNESS, Story 65
TRUST, Stories 9, 20, 23, 34, 61
WISDOM, Stories 33, 37, 50, 66